"This book is brilliant! It feels warm, friendly and safe and it's going to be a fantastic resource for survivors."
— A Survivor

"Absolutely brilliant!! I just love everything about it - heartbreaking and inspiring and conveys that sense of sisterhood through the shared experience."
— A Survivor

"All professionals that women could potentially have to interact with should be far better informed of the complexities of domestic abuse and narcissists. This book is a brilliant way to take them 'there' in a way they wouldn't otherwise be able to. An incredibly useful resource for professionals and I'll most definitely be promoting the hell out of it!"
— Christine El Issa,
Family social worker and women's life coach

"I would highly recommend this book to other therapists working in the area of narcissistic abuse, to get a feel for the depth and breadth of women's experiences, and to be able to offer clients an additional resource to explore and support their therapy. It's certainly on my bookshelf!"
— Charlotte Pardy,
Psychotherapist MA Cert Soc Sci Dip mBACP reg

My Red Quilt

Women survivors of narcissistic abuse
re-writing their stories, from heartbreak to
hope and healing

Edited by
Sally Olewe-Richards, PhD
with Stephanie Kerber

**Women of Wisdom
and Courage®**

womenofwisdomandcourage.com

CONTENTS

From One Warrior to Another
by Tamson Sherlock

Although you don't know me
I would like to remind you
That you are such a beautiful soul
Inside and out

Whatever you are facing right now
I promise
There is light at the end of the tunnel

You are an incredibly strong woman
With such courage
I know it's not easy
I know you are probably tired
Hurting and exhausted

But remember
When things get hard
To take deep breaths
Count to 10
Look into the mirror

And tell yourself, "I've got this.
I am strong, I am loved
And I am needed.
Better days are coming"

You're not alone
The world needs your beautiful smile
You might not heal today
Tomorrow or next month
But I promise
When you do
It will all be worth it.

Janet Rose: 'Love Yourself'

Introduction

"The poetic mind is the root of change. We'll always look to poets for the beginning of true transformation... to place beauty at the forefront of what they are feeling, even when they are expressing the pain of their life experience"
—Jacqueline Suskin, author of *Every Day Is a Poem*

These pages contain 80 poems and 20 original pieces of art, which have been created and generously contributed by 50 courageous women. These women range in age from their 20's to early 70's. Their voices come from all over the world - Nigeria, USA, Australia, Greece, Kenya, Canada, Wales, Scotland, England, Republic of Ireland, Mexico, New Zealand and the Philippines. Although they may never meet in person, what connects them is that they've all endured suffering at the hands of an abusive, narcissistic partner.

The powerful poems they share in this book are testament to their strength and willingness to fight for themselves and a better life. The rallying cry of a global sisterhood, coming together through shared pain to rise up and reclaim their lives.

We're humbled and honoured they trusted us to include their work in this book and that you have made the decision to use it as a healing resource on your own recovery journey.

We thank you all, from the bottom of our hearts.

The Power of Poetry

Many people find that writing poetry is therapeutic for them, particularly during and after trauma. It's a way of revisiting events from a safe place, helping the writer to make sense of what has happened to them, to express how they felt and are feeling now, and to find and state their inner strength, ultimately helping them to come to terms and eventually heal from their trauma.

Poetry can be time travel; it can transport the reader into our personal world so that they see what we saw, hear what we heard, feel exactly how we felt. Poetry can be sorrowful and through it we can mourn for what we have lost, and metaphorically heal our wounds. Poetry can be hugely cathartic, it can make sense of events that may have seemed mystifying at the time and it can release strong or difficult emotions that were trapped and had no other outlet. Poetry can be angry and defiant; it can be an amazing medium for freeing ourselves from trauma that kept us fearful and weak; it can affirm ourselves as strong, resilient people and it can let us be heard when perhaps we have not been allowed to speak. Finally, poetry can be gentle and healing and through it we can learn to love ourselves and move towards a hopeful future. The poems in this book express all these things and more.

The idea for the book came after a number of women shared poems about their experiences in the online narcissistic abuse support community, Women of Wisdom and Courage®. Together with being cathartic for the women sharing their poems, what was striking was how their words were able to speak directly to the lived experiences and shared pain of other women in the group, making them feel they were "understood", "not crazy", "not alone" and "heard without speaking".

This type of connection through a community of shared lived experience holds immense healing power. Indeed, Johann Hari has said, "*The opposite of addiction is not sobriety, it's connection*". If we're struggling to break free from the addictive dynamics of these abusive relationships (often referred to as the 'trauma bond'), having a community of women who understand our struggles, who will hold space for our pain, without judgement, is hugely powerful. However, not all women wish to or are able to access online support groups. This gave Women of Wisdom and Courage® founder, Dr Sally Olewe-Richards, the idea to publish an anthology of survivors' poetry to bring these words of understanding, hope and healing to other women that may need to hear them.

A call for poetry submissions was shared within the community in September 2020 and published author and poet, Stephanie Kerber, was invited to run an online poetry writing workshop for women who wanted to write, but perhaps didn't know where to start. A comment that we often heard after people sent their poems in for this book, was that the writers had indeed found it therapeutic to express their thoughts and feelings in words. In fact, one woman told us, "*It's the most therapeutic and empowering thing I've ever done in my life*".

This insight led to the book evolving into more than 'just' an anthology, and it is now also an invitation and guide for readers to write about their own experiences as a way to heal the pain and injustices they've suffered. In doing so, by giving a voice to those things abusers work so hard to keep hidden, we may even be able to create a sense of *poetic justice*.

All poems have remained as close to the original submission as possible and any edits have been done with the consent and collaboration of the author. A number of women submitted artwork for the book, which due to printing costs, are featured here in black and white. However, originals will be uploaded, with the artist's permission, to the Women of Wisdom and Courage® website for readers to see them in their true, original versions.

The book is divided into three sections:

Her Story holds the words these inspiring women wanted to share with you. The poems are arranged to reflect the journey we go on after surviving an abusive relationship, especially if it has been with someone displaying traits ascribed to the more extreme end of the Narcissism Spectrum Scale.

Dance with the Devil *tells the story of how we become entangled in these relationships and the damage they do to us through the onslaught of physical, psychological, sexual and financial abuses that so often happen.*

At the Crossroads *describes the point where we realise we can no longer stay and need to make the heartbreaking - and possibly dangerous - decision to leave. The crossroads can also be the internal struggle to let go of pain and false hope, if we have been discarded.*

Broken Wings *brings into heart-wrenching clarity the often-experienced aftermath of PTSD, depression, anxiety, flashbacks, nightmares and a myriad of other conditions, which survivors are so often left to cope with, after they have broken free physically.*

Never Again *includes poems fuelled by righteous anger, defiance and a commitment to not let the narcissistic abuser 'win'. They are testament to the strength and courage of women to rise up, heal and reclaim their lives once more.*

And Here, I Will Fly shows that you should always keep hope alive because real healing is possible. It's time to re-write your story and choose the ending you deserve. The title for this book, and inspiration for the cover artwork, draw on the beautiful words and imagery of the poem 'My Red Quilt' by K. Christy Moore, found at the end of this section.

Your Story explains why expressive writing is such a powerful recovery tool and invites you to begin exploring, understanding and releasing your own pain, through journaling and poetry. We recognise that writing poetry may not be familiar or comfortable for everyone, so we provide a brief guide on how you can begin exploring it for yourself. We hope this will help you to use poetry to tell your story and be a healing, strengthening and liberating tool for you and your recovery.

Our Story provides more context about Women of Wisdom and Courage®, the global sisterhood for narcissistic abuse recovery. Readers are invited to send their poems to be shared on the website, creating an on-going, living, breathing 'conversation' between survivors from around the world.

"You're not a victim for sharing your story. You are a survivor setting the world on fire with your truth. And you never know who needs your light, your warmth and raging courage"
- Alex Elle

Her Story

Dance with the Devil

Journeys
by K. Christy Moore

Girl
If someone comes journeying into your heart
And promises adventures
Check carefully the itinerary
And the end destination
You may need to pack a helmet and shield
Rather than shorts and sandals
It may not be a passport you need
But a lantern to find your way
Back to yourself and home
After a long journey down
Dark lanes.

The Mask
by Melanie Isaac

Your smirks
I catch from the corner of my eye
Fleeting flashes of your true self
So fast before the mask returns
The mask that keeps me
The paper cuts of humiliation
Poison darts of manipulations
The crashing whisper of intimidation

It was all there from the start but
You kept the sound down so low
It was easy to miss right then

I have learnt all of these words
In the past four years

Gaslighting
Triangulation
Hypervigilance
Narcissist

You took away my lust for living
But inspired me to write again

Now I know what a predator looks like
Now I know it looks like you.

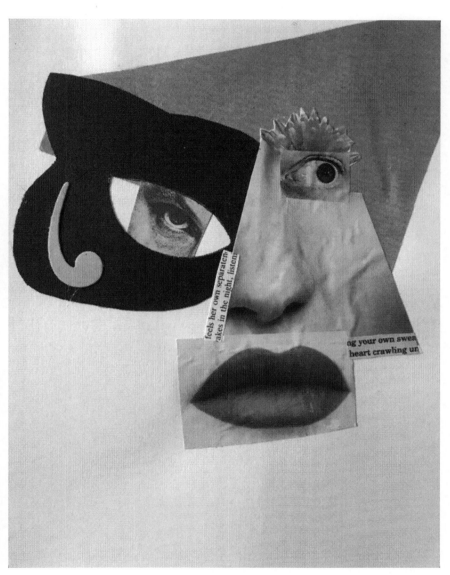

Chloe Miller: 'Mask'

The Cycle
by Villy Tentoma Zervou

Excited
High in dopamine
Complimented
Given attention
Time
Energy
Flattered
Mesmerised
In lust
Submitted
Admired

In passion
Intense feelings
Motivated
Positivity
Negativity
Driven

Feeling seen
Feeling heard
Feeling valued
In love
Obsessed
Hooked
Dominated
Put down
Not enough
Shown contempt
Blamed
Shamed
Judged
Criticised
Compared

Attacked
Worthless
Devalued
Isolated
Brainwashed
Confused
Alone
Lonely
Scared
Coerced
Controlled
Manipulated

Gaslighted
Push-pull
Labelled
Diagnosed
Hurt
Disappointed
Regretted
Remorseful
Guilty
Misunderstood
Walking on eggshells

Punished
Withdrawn
Withheld
Neglected
Used
Deprived
Exploited
Ignored
Abused
Rejected
Abandoned

Discarded

Hoovered

Hopeful

Wishfully thinking
In denial
Confused
Cognitive dissonance
Addicted

All over again
Trauma Bonded.

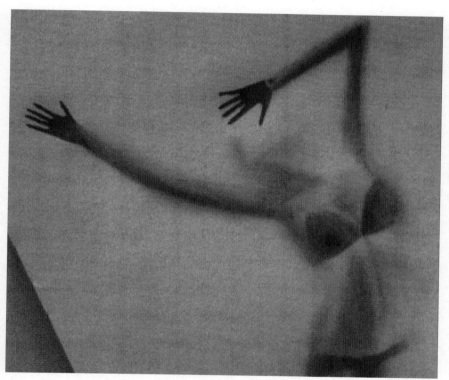

Róisín Smyth: "I painted this when I was 19 years old and felt trapped in an abusive relationship.

Why Didn't She Leave Sooner?
by Grace Louise

Today, I tried to leave
Today, he put his children in front of me
To explain why I was leaving
He knew I would not do this
Today, I did not leave

Today, I tried to leave
I packed the essentials and had them in my car
Walking out the door, he walked in the door
Anger
Fury
Smashing
Today, I did not leave

Today, I tried to leave
He blocked the doorway and trapped me inside
Today, I did not leave

Today, I tried to leave
He loves me, he is going to change
It was just an accident
Today, I did not leave

Today, I tried to leave
Chest puffed, shouting in my face
I hide in the spare room
Today, I did not leave

Today, I tried to leave
A bottle of wine and numerous tablets
I left by ambulance
He came to the hospital
Lies
Home
Today, I did not leave

Today, I tried to leave
"No-one will love you
You are a slut
You are a waste of space
I am the best you will ever get"
Belief
Today, I did not leave

Today, I was brave
Today, I was courageous
Today, I saved myself

Today, I left

"But why didn't you leave sooner?" they ask.

A Letter to Myself, From My Ex
by Alison Romero

Alison,

I enticed you into my pitfall of dark, impure, and insidious
    psychotic hell
With my seemingly trusting and doting charisma
A deception of disguise and tainted lies.

I propelled you to an absolute height of euphoric ecstasy
Only to have you plunge, spiralling
Into a million broken pieces of self-destruction
And along the way, losing your soul
And sacrificing your loved ones.

Now, you dare me to feel an ounce of pathetic remorse towards
    you;
I won't, '**AS I KNOW WHAT I DO, AND IT PLEASES AND
    EXALTS ME**'
I expect you to grovel and beg for my validation and deservingness
And I continuously bash you in ways you could not even
    conceivably imagine.

But, instead, you found strength, sought truth and discovered–
Me, for who I truly am... a coward, who uses and defies others
Who puts on a mask of deceit in public
But behind the doors of my domain
I am cruel, evil, spiteful, selfish, and all that is despicable and
    loathsome
And above all, I cheat, lie, and intimidate
Leaving emotional scars deeply embedded

For it is I who am undeserving of those who are good, kind and in
    God's favour.
You mean nothing to me, nor my children
No one, as I never fought to hold on to any of you
And someday, I will mean nothing to everyone

Your Ex.

In the Safety of His Control
by Clare Swift

In the safety of his control
Often feels the cosier place to be
Rather than in some social gathering
Or mingling with family

Due to his disliking of
My far away engagements
His games will begin
Only to your amazement
The toying of my emotions and attachments
Send me into despair
He plays with every heart string
'Til I'm pulling out my hair

I take a step of courage and say "Hey, what the hell"
Haven't seen my friends in ages and
They want to see me as well
My smile is there to greet them and the old
Me they dearly know
But they can't see the stirring that goes on deep below

Have I kept him happy, did I answer all the calls?
I'm meant to be sipping tea but I feel like running down the halls
It's becoming unbearable as I see my life has changed
A call to meet a friend feels like I'm wrapped up in chains

I find that inner confidence and tell myself I'll stand strong
But when the invites come flooding in I know where I belong
Lock that cage nicely and there I'll sit and wait
'Cos then at least I know and it's familiar
What will be served upon my plate
Control is a dish served often and I wonder if he has no true idea
That he's made my world so unkind and full of comfortable fear.

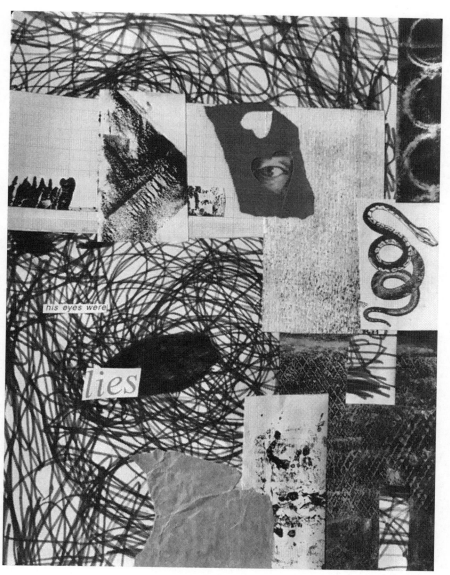

Chloe Miller: 'His Eyes Were Lies'

Dance With the Devil
by Hilary Daw

Shall we dance – you and I?
Shall we dance under the moonlit sky?
Will we waltz under the stars
My smile hiding my scars?
My hopes, my dreams, my life on hold
Where my soul has been bought and sold

Will you leave my heart in tatters?
My sad reflection in a glass that so easily shatters
My invisible wounds that run so deep
My brain that just can't sleep
The peace I so desperately crave
My low expectations when once I was so brave

Shall we tango to your tune?
Whilst you whisper that you're leaving soon?
Will you destroy my life
When once I couldn't wait to be your wife?
The tangle of sheets, where my heart no longer beats
The love I thought was there
Then I realised you just don't care

Will we quickstep round our issue
While I look for compassion within you?
Will I find what I am looking for?
A consistent cup from which I pour?
A look, a touch, a dance of pleasure
A relationship that I can treasure

Or will I pirouette alone
On the sands where we once roamed?
My father, my husbands, my lovers, my brother
The men I know are all one another

I dance to my tune as the waves tickle my feet
The music in my head now has a different beat
I'm free and my soul feels pure
My dance with the devil is over, for sure.

A Prayer to God for Justice
by Joanna Grace L. Barretto

(original written in Tagalog and translated into English)

Is there anything more painful than the disease of abuse
Staining your personality?
How many years have you been suffering
And being tested inside?

Prayer to the Lord God of Justice:
"Lord God
When will I greet you?
For how long will I endure the pain
And painful words spoken to me?
Listen to God, the Father" is my cry.

Tired and troubled mood, let it be peace
My personality continues to be attacked with harsh feelings
Irritation and disobedience familiar to me

"You Oh God are truly just
I suffer this and need your help
Do not neglect others' oppression
Take care of me
My heart is full of tears and mercy
Grant me justice and be a good example
Take me in your arms
My mind is light so it won't be in danger
Forgive me and let me feel your care
For in your love and mercy
You, Oh God, are truly great!
In you I will continue to trust."

The Heart and the Brain
by Olivia Blake

"Are you still awake?" asked the brain
"Yes, Wife" said the heart
"I've been right all along" said the brain
"I know, Wife" said the heart
"He lies so much" said the brain
"That's true, Wife" said the heart
"He manipulates and steals" said the brain
"You're right, Wife" said the heart
"I don't know what I am going to do" said the brain
"But it has been this way all along, Wife" said the heart
"Did you know?" asked the brain
"Yes, Wife, I knew" said the heart
"Why didn't I see it?" asked the brain
"Look at your children, Mother" said the heart
"I don't understand" said the brain
"Stay Mother" said the heart
"I don't know if I can bear this" said the brain
"Don't go, Mother" said the heart
"I'm so tired" said the brain
"Rest, then, Mother" said the heart
"Goodnight" said the brain
"Goodnight, Mother" said the heart.

He Never Hit Me
By Jade Holmes

He screamed in my face
But he didn't hit me

He punched the wall
But he didn't hit me

He told me I was useless
But he didn't hit me

He wouldn't allow me to see my family
But he didn't hit me

He checked my phone
But he didn't hit me

He tracked my location
But he didn't hit me

He called me stupid, ugly and a whore
But he didn't hit me

He told me he was the only one that would put up with me
But he didn't hit me

He made me feel guilty for not wanting to have sex
But he didn't hit me

He humiliated me in front of people
But he didn't hit me

He refused to help with the children
But he didn't hit me

He controlled my finances
But he didn't hit me

He made me hate myself
But he never hit me.

Mirrors
by Tina M. Durbin

We look in them each morning
To see who we are presenting to the world
We look at our eyes and our hair and our teeth
We style our clothes
And we make sure each hair is in place
We put on jewellery to draw attention to our style
And we smile as others compliment us
We shy away as they admire our clothes and our hair
Our jewellery and our fashion sense ...
Because we know none of this is the reflection we want the world
To truly see

We want the world to see us as US
But all we often see
Is how we THINK the world sees us

We smile when we don't want to
We believe when it seems too good
We support when we love another
We mirror to the world
What we wish the world mirrored back

And then .... Along comes a mirror who admits his cracks
And says he doesn't need every hair in place
He admires your flaws and sees you as a blessing
Despite your outer dressing
He says all the right things
And he brings you flowers
He seems to be the change you've been waiting for
And he encourages you
To be more than you ever saw in the mirror

As you stand in front of that mirror
Your reflection frown becomes a crown of glory and
You believe in what he says he sees
Your reflection is a woman who is strong
And beautiful
Your outside shows the inside
And you glow
As you glow
The glitter shines
In the silver of the mirror

Just when the mirror inside
Matches the mirror outside
A crack begins to appear in the corner
It widens and deepens
As the crevice in the mirror grows longer
The man who said he saw everything
Now says he sees nothing
The man who said he loved your flaws
Now sees them as reasons of anxiety
He sees your shared vulnerabilities
And insecurities
As weaknesses
And he reflects them daily
As he throws them up to your face

When you look in the mirror
The cracks begin to creep across your face
As you trace each fallen tear
Each tear is a fear that has replaced
The beauty once seen in the mirror

As you strain to find a glimpse
Of the woman in the mirror
Who loved the flaws of the man
Who loved your unpolished finish
You realise
He simply mirrored you to gaze upon your jewels
As you gave
He took
But as he took
You gave
And you lost the look
Of a man who never saw you

The truth is
The mirror only reflects what it sees
When you see a stronger woman
It isn't a reflection of what another sees
But instead it is what you are reflecting
When a man mirrors your strengths
He is seeing into your soul

Don't be fooled by what shines and glitters
As others see your crown
But instead be impressed
By the man who reflects his own crown

Then and only then can a King and a Queen
Truly reflect to the world
A kingdom of royalty
Love and loyalty.

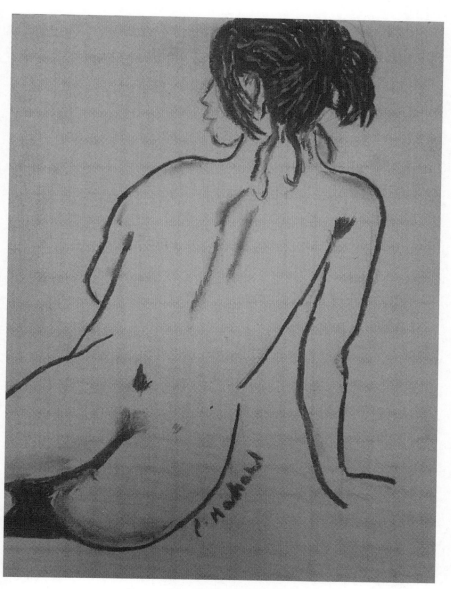

Penny Marshall: 'Vulnerability'

What Do You Do?
by Stephanie Kerber

What do you do
When you break open
The bones of you and lay them bare?
The delicate marrow waiting there
Expectant
Receptive
Accepting
Dependent
Shivering softly in the cool grey
Of a nondescript impassive day

What do you do
When a restless, playful Autumn breeze
Swoops, chuckling with the scent of forests and seas
Rushes past you to pull up the skirts of the trees
And reckless, scatters
Stars and bones and leaves?

Do you sigh?
Do you hide your face
In the pillows of the sky?
Do you pick up your bones
And cry and lay them out again upon your bed?
Does the tune of a lament
Echo around your silent lips and in your brimming head?

Yes. Yes, all those things and so much more
But you shake out the curtains and sweep the floor
And arrange your bones
Beneath the welcome mat by the open door
You live, you smile, you hide the tears and hope
And you cope
And you cope
And you cope

If someone would ever take the time to truly look
Through your fragile bones
Into the open book
Of your patient, loving eyes
They would see what you really do
They would see the bones of you
Picking up the rainbow paint
Making your mark, subtle and faint
Writing endless joy against the maelstrom
Of the low and stormy skies.

This is Apparently Love
by Raffaela

I was a 'cunt' again last night
Not sure what I did this time
Other than be me
The same person I was when we met
The same person he was so keen to
Be his girlfriend

I think it might have been something
To do with me dancing? Yeah
I remember
I remember me dancing being some
Kind of issue
Yep
Dancing!
What the actual fuck!?

In not even a year I've been an
'attention seeker'
A 'bully'
A 'dickhead' more times than I could
Shake a stick at
I'm often 'weird'
And 'horrible'
And 'mean'

I've been shouted at
For fuck all

I've been sent to Coventry
At the end of the night
Countless times
For imagined crimes
And this is apparently love

"I love you" he says
All the time
But you don't call someone you love
A cunt

For dancing.

The Sun
by Rola Mahmoud

Day after day you shall know
That everything comes then goes
Yet what is so clear
A tear in her eyes
Or in her heart fear

Life keeps going on
Someone is born
Someone is gone

Trying to smile at the sun of a new day
Sending its lovely golden ray
Trying and trying
Yet, what can I do
When my heart is full of fears more than I can bear?

Are the answers to many more questions with you?
I want to laugh, to smile
But I do not dare.

The Fall
by Kirsty Hutchinson

I became the burning fuel
For his narcissistic grin
Repeatedly climbing the walls
As the ceiling above me was caving in

I couldn't see the light
In my tunnel of dark and dread
The madness lost inside of me
A battle between heart and head

The raging monster pressed me
Die, or dare to try and win
Until only a ghost was left of me
And darkness escaped from within.

Ruth Woodcock: 'Is This Love?'

She Holds Her Water
by Valena

There is a tree
She stays silent
Amid the arid yellow ground
She remembers splendour!
Roots that curl beneath her
Aching at the day's end
Reaching downward
Afraid to look up

Her branches, they say
Are weeping
She sprouts another
And another, hurriedly
Reaching for the sky
Searching for the sun, until
She droops and holds her water
To find daylight once again

Heat! Too strong, burning
Yearning to see, feel
Anything but the life
That is.

At the Crossroads

To Kindness
by Anonymous

I'm a grump and feel crazy because of it all
But I'll never regret the softness that exists inside me
When I remained silent after being yelled and sworn at in public
For embracing him anyways...
For forgiving him and trying to see the good in him
Regardless of being called names hundreds of times

I simply state his actions to show that this softness is not easy
And it always loves him
I still want to show that love and help him see me again in person
The softness realizes it's wrong after what he's done
Over and over again
Kindness gives and gives
And I don't regret any moment of silence
Of being alone after the storm
And the hundreds of tears and thoughts of death

To have been able to hold him and feel his soul!
I wouldn't trade it back
To feel his vulnerability
The years of pain were worth it
To still love and see the worth of him
I'd never trade the softness in

He has feelings too
And he can be soft too
But even kindness has to let others go

Oh, how I've fallen but I will stand.

I See You
by Michelle N. Opel

I see you in there
Little boy
Little one whose mom
Isn't there like she could be
Like she should be

I see you in there
Scared little boy
Looking back at me through
Grown man eyes
Putting on a brave face
Ashamed to let anyone see
Yourself

But I see you, precious one
The real you
And I want to love you well
I want to love you whole

So I rush in
Wrap you in my skin of unselfishness
My arms of adoring acceptance
Trading pieces of my life
For shards of your pain
My essence oozing out
As I lay it on your altar

If I just do enough, give enough, love enough
Be enough
If I just die enough
You'll be whole

You'll be wholly who I needed
You'll be wholly who I love
You'll be wholly and completely different
Than the scared little boy
Watching me bleed
Watching me die
While he holds the knife

Oh, precious one
I loved you well
But I can't love you whole.

I Know
by Penny Marshall

Tomorrow will be better
Tomorrow will be calm
If only I try harder
But I can feel the sweat in my palm

I've done it again
I've pushed him too far
My punishment is silence
He heads for the bar

He tells me I'm selfish
I only think of me
But I try so hard
So how can this be?

His words cut deep
They feel too true
My family and friends say
You are no longer you

But I must try harder
I can't let him go
My friends don't understand
I tell them I know

I know I must leave
I know I can't stay
But I can't find the strength
There is just no way

There is no way I can leave
I love him too much
I can't imagine life without him
I'm weak to his touch

He tells me he loves me
He says I'm his all
But as night time falls
I just stare at the wall

He's drinking too much
He promised to stop
I want to believe him
But he just needs his crutch

I know I must leave him
I know I can't stay
But I can't find the strength
There is just no way

But I'm starting to change
I feel strength from within
Now I'm in control
Of when my new life will begin.

Stuck
by Róisín Smyth

Low serotonin
I felt so alone in
That house, my head
A battle that I'll never win
I just give up instead

I need sedating
It's detonating
This anxiety
Inside my body, dominating
It has a hold of me
Chest compressing
So depressing

Wanna disappear
Stop messing with my head
I'm stressing
All I feel is fear

Society won't silence me
Conditioning my brain
Making me feel insane
I will not be medicated
For your financial gain
This really is more complicated
There's reasons for this pain
Invisible ball and chain
My body's breaking from the strain
I'm always to blame
In your big game
I'm the target
Waiting for you to take aim

The bloodstains
I wash them off in the rain
It's like a hurricane
Out here

But I've got to get away.

At the Crossroads
by Jenney Moore

So many years
Your cruelty oppresses
Oceans of tears
No relent nor remorse

I am forced now
To the crossroads

There was a time
You seemed a god
All was a rhyme
You shone like sunlight

I did not see
The looming crossroads

The expanse of pain
I live in a cage
No shelter from rain
More false explanations

I must go now
Facing the crossroads

Cutting you away
You'll never care
Not under your sway
I'm awakened now

Square my shoulders
At the crossroads

Standing up straight
Clarity of vision
Freed from your hate
I'm ready at last

I'll choose SANITY
At the crossroads.

Yesterday – The Story of Freedmum
by Freedmum

Yesterday, I used to dream that today would be such a good day as it was in the beginning

Yesterday, I dreamt that I would be good enough and you would be the great guy that I met

Yesterday, I used to dream that it would be like at the start, when you did everything for me

Yesterday, I dreamt that it would be so amazing, just like in the first days

Yesterday, I wept tears that stung my cheeks, like the strongest nettle, but just wiped away unnoticed, hiding my shame

Yesterday, I sobbed silently as every drop of pain shook my body, hidden by my laughter, loud and raucous

Yesterday, the hidden drops of rage fell so violently, burning my eyes like a poker scorching my soul, yet veiled by smile

Yesterday, the pain in my eyes was concealed by my mask, so expertly worn every day

Yesterday, your harsh words shattered my heart into fragments; scattered across the room, hidden in every crevice, nook and cranny, never to be found again

Yesterday, those mocking, scornful words echoed in every room, dragging me down into your pool of anger and drowning me in your waves of rage

Yesterday, your sardonic smile deceived the world with your charm and wit, as you fooled me so many times

Yesterday, your bitter blows cut me through to the core, so expertly chopping me down, just as a tree is felled with one crashing blow

Yesterday, the room was dark, hidden shadows in every corner, concealing your next move

Yesterday, the world was black hiding the way to the light, despite the glorious sunshine and cloudless sky

Yesterday, the rain drummed against the window like the constant hammering of your put-downs and scathing comments

Yesterday, the snow lay frozen on the ground hiding the beauty of the earth, oh the irony of your beautiful face hiding a vile, frozen soul

Yesterday, the time that is no more, gone but never to be forgotten

Yesterday, the time has given me today, time to heal my pain and scars

Yesterday has given me tomorrow to live and be free.

Escape
by Penny Marshall

I stare at the wall
The writing was there
I chose to ignore it
It was too much to bear

I feel the confusion
My mind I don't know
He says he loves me
But I think it's just show

His words can be sweet
He turns on the charm
One step out of line
My heart feels the harm

I said I was bored
His anger rose up
I saw hate in his eyes
This is all so fucked up

The cracks they were there
Right from the start
But his loving words
Spoke straight to my heart

I wanted to feel love
At the beginning I did
It was all so perfect
You kept your true self well hid

On I went
Convincing myself
Far more scared
To be left on the shelf

If I try harder
All his problems I can solve
I just needed to focus
Or our love would dissolve

As the years passed by
Things they got worse
I was starting to think
I was under a curse

I knew in my heart
I just needed to find
The strength from within
To myself I must be kind

I needed to think
I knew I was right
My mind was getting clearer
I was ready to put up a fight

You see the cracks they just grow
They don't disappear
I knew in my heart
My escape was near!

Girl, Jump!
by K. Christy Moore

Yes, the jump is terrifying
The obstacles obscured
The landing only hoped for
You long for a map, a light
A parachute

But truth be told
You only grow wings
Once you take the leap
And only your wings
Can save you.

What a Day
by Michelle N. Opel

It's so easy
Comfortable, familiar
To abandon myself
To forget I exist, I matter
To project my love
And believe I have something good
When I receive little regard in return

Oh what a day
When I realize I project
All my goodness
My light, my love, my loyalty
Oh what a day
When I realize I do have a good thing
I have ME.

Ruth Woodcock: 'Your Future Is At Your Fingertips'

Raining Tears No More
by Cara Wiseman

And the sadness resonates
And seeps through
Like sodden denim in a downpour
No matter how big the raincoat or the size of the heart
When realisation came it shook my bones to the core
Like the rotten fence in the storm
Not shielding, not keeping it out

And when acceptance comes
There'll be my resolve
like a break in the clouds
Or a light growing closer to a sailor lost at sea.

Once a Wife
by V. Oake

Tonight is the last night
A page to turn right over
Hopefully luck will follow
Like a little four-leaf clover

I will have to live without my children
For at least an empty chunk of time
I feel a void, sad and lost
Like I'm committing the most heinous crime

I know the short term will be hard
A mourning of a past life
For once upon a time
I promised to be the best wife

I know I have to move right on
No time to look back and think
This is my time to shine
And not allow myself to sink.

Survival
by Olivia Blake

S taying won't change anything
M ake a plan to go
I t's only going to get worse
L eave when you have found a safe place
E scape.

Adrift
by Olivia Blake

A

           D

   R

                     I

     F

        T

S

  C

A

        TT

   E

     R

E

                  D

J

   U

      S

T

F

   L

          Y

Janet Rose: 'Time to Fly'

Love
by K. Christy Moore

Love is but a thousand deaths
Some slow, some quick like your
Breath as you run
Each dream, a child you birth
Raise and watch stumble, walk then run
Or die

As we spend our time changing, yearning
The pain of each discord is a sentence
To who we are
How do you know when to fight or
When to give up;
If the end is worth the journey?
We must follow our heart.

Truth is Freedom
by Mary Wride

I know the truth, but refuse to see it
I have an inner guide, but don't heed her
I am free to choose, but prefer denial
I say 'yes', but there is a bigger 'no'

I am not who I think I am

I am already free

My life can be different.

Broken Wings

You Are a Curse
by Cara Wiseman

If I call out to the moon enough, will it bring you back to me?
For I'd cast whatever spell, hex or curse
Just to have you return
And not our love in the ashes burn

Because I miss you
And my heart, now shrunken, still yearns
For someone other than you
Since you turned my heart blue

The time is now or once was, it's lost
Never was, could've been...

I don't want to keep writing poems about you.

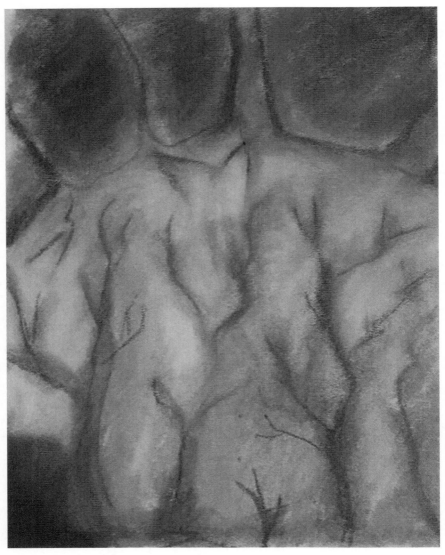

Andi G: "I created this at a time I was feeling frustrated. I was in the middle of being pushed and pulled with a custody situation with my narcissist ex and his kids' mom. It was a horrible time; this feeling of everything building up like fire and having no place to go".

Likeable
by Njoki B.

A majority want to be liked
Appreciated and loved
No wonder it hurts so much
When one faces rejection
From the ones they loved

I wake up hurting
I hurt in my dreams
I go through it over and over again

Waiting for time
To heal my painful memories

Soon.

PART ONE: Broken Wings
by Yvette Bruni

What happened to this person that stands before me?
What happened to her beautiful soul
That has been ripped and torn by emotional turmoil?
A silent voice whispered
"I'm sorry, but you changed and not for the good I'm afraid to say"

A few voices told me my life
Would not be good with you in it
They captured the essence of the truth
I didn't see it for a long time
Although the messages were plain to see
Clear as water and loud as a nuclear bomb

You see they were right
I did change. It was painful to see the person I had become
As a result of being with you

My whole being had changed
Not all of me!
I still held on to my compassion and dignity
People would remind me of who I really was
And the person I had become
But you tore away my true identity
With your being and presence
Ripped it away from my being
You wore me down until I was just an empty shell
A butterfly with broken wings

I never knew a person like you could exist
Naivety was the ace card
You fuelled my anger
I was embarrassed by this
Catastrophe ruled my world
It became a badge
Not of honour, but of convenience

I was ashamed most of the time
Ashamed that my life took this awkward turning
And I couldn't find my way
I was lost at the crossroads
Didn't know which way to turn
Which road to take
Guided hands stretched out to me
But beyond my reach
I desperately wanted to grab them and not let go

I managed once or twice
But then like a cyclone I was swallowed back
Into a life of chaos
I would always tell myself
The good outweighed the bad
Somehow downplay what was really going on
Like playing my favourite record
Over and over again
And finding myself back at square one.
I threw you lifelines so many times
But I never had an anchor
To stop the destruction

But here I stand
A butterfly with broken wings
How long will it take?
I whisper to those helping hands
How long for the pain to subside?
For the words to stop?

Like a clock that has forgotten to chime.

Never Love
by Kim Alexandra

You
Who promised me everything and said that we were special

Me
Who showed you all my truths and needed only kindness

We
Were brief and loving and broken and dreamers and the worst and
the best and the most

Love
Was it love? Was it ever love? It was never love, just games, abuse
and lies

Gone
Forever now, what that was. That tainted love that never was. That
fierce and blinding never love

Scar
That left this place inside of me that hurts from you and aches for
you and may never fall again.

Shattered Dream
by Louise de la Haye

I dreamt of a happy family life
When you asked me to be your wife

You were charming, fit and strong
How could my choice prove to be so wrong?

I thought you would love and protect me
But that didn't turn out to be

I ignored the flags coloured red
Until you did so much damage inside my head

I've ended up with PTSD
Now that's my life, that's me

Nothing can change what happened to me
In a crisis I went through called "DV"

I still freeze with fear
Anytime you are near

I'd love my old self to one day return
Mindfulness and meditation is something I am trying to learn

To help me out of the pain
Enabling me to feel again

I hope I will heal one day
That the nightmares and flashbacks will go away

Until that time comes along
I just have to be incredibly strong.

Skye: "This is a significant image I painted when I was immensely missing my daughter. After I had left, I had nowhere to live, so had to let him take my daughter back"

Skin Interrupted
by Kate Sanderson

The heartbreak in that cut
As failure leaks and oozes down your arm

Red water reproaches me

I dress and bind more than skin
I bandage love.

Survive Safe and Alive or Thrive?
by Frances A. Rove

"What doesn't kill you makes you stronger..."
There is that survivor badge I didn't want to earn
Let alone gather into a collection
Tell God I'm strong enough, I'm tough
Stop! Enough!

It is true that I am no longer a martyr to my memories
But what doesn't kill you can make you resilient and hypervigilant

Now is a time for peace and mindful meditation
To allow the flashbacks to flow away
It's time for therapy and me

We all get stones in our lives
We can choose to construct a bridge to help others
A wall to repel them
Or an altar to thank God for our survival
My stones are numerous and heavy
I don't want to merely throw them in rageful revenge
But I do not yet know what I have the strength to build

Maybe the weight of those stones kills the original personality
So that you can become the survivor you were meant to be

I'd love to write a memoir about my journey –
To help those who know narcissism, trauma, enmeshment, sexual
    abuse, mood disorders
But am I strong enough to help anyone but myself?
Am I too thin-skinned for sniping book reviews and negative
    comments online?

Did my life really make me stronger or use me up?
Did it leave me with a desire to protect myself
From even the stress of telling my story and risking more
   negativity?

It didn't kill me, but it went on long and unabated
And maybe I'm not a survivor but a hollowed-out husk
But I am safe
Like the ship in the dock
And I want to stay safe
But they say ships are not made for the safety of the dock

Do I really want to write my story as a good example of growth and
   change
When I still feel fragile and damaged?
Is a work in progress good enough to help someone else
To go on, survive and thrive?

I know we are all works in progress
But have I progressed enough to write and take what comes?
Or is self-preservation too dear now
So my story must die as I live on anonymously
Stronger, but safe?

I Died a Little Today
by Tricia Merten

I died a little today
That part of you that believes
God never gives you more than you can handle

That part of you that believes
We are stronger than we know and will overcome

That part of you that believes
In the end only kindness matters and love conquers all

That huge, big part that drives, sustains
And keeps on believing that I'll rise up

I didn't rise up today
I spent the entire day in my room
Curled up in bed, foetal position
Trying to calm the horrible, raging pit in my stomach
Where my heart dropped into

And the searing pain
As the acid eroded away my citadel stronghold
And made me, for the first time in a very, very long time
Feel like there was no purpose or meaning to my existence

That if I could, without fear of disgracing my family
Or without guilt for causing them pain
I would pray for sleep to pull me deep down into the abyss
Where my heart already resides
And cover my ears, my eyes, my mouth and shroud me in darkness
To never awaken again

I died a little today
When I thought of promises and pain
And wishing time could rewind
So we could re-enact not one or two or three scenes
But the whole chapter of that part of our lives
Where we made a mess of something that could have been
So pure and wonderful and magical

I died a little today
When I couldn't find that centre core that gives you
The gumption to stand tall and fight the fight

The crusader-cloaked army strength
That points its glistening steel shaft at the shadows looming
    overhead
All around

That voice of reasoning and reckoning
That I am not this day that stifles the life
From my pulsating veins

That I am not the whole of this cataclysmic surge
That sucks the air from my lungs because
The pain has made it impossible to breathe

I died a little today
When I swallowed what I hoped would be my lifeline
Chasing it down with an unadulterated gulp of yearning
That the waves constantly crashing over my body, my mind, my
    soul
Causing the tremors to unfold repeatedly over and over again
Would stop

I died a little today
As the piercing point of reality's arrow plunged into my being
And I cried the toxic demons from my body
While the spasms took their toll on my strength and reserve
Retching the oxymoronic thought that life could want you to die

I died a little today
When I thought I could remember what joy felt like
When laughter kissed her lips with such deep desperation
And appreciation for the beauty that resounds there
Echoing into the chasms of this life wind that surrounds us
And blows away that heartache and despair
And whispers into the air
"This too shall pass"

But it did not pass
This feeling of lost languished promises and dreams
And hopes and fanciful idealism
That love truly is the most important
That of these three that remain: Faith, Hope and Love
The greatest of these is Love

I died a little today at the thought of you.

Natasha Wright: 'A self-portrait during and after these relationships.'

I Am Not Me Anymore
by Tricia Merten

Joy - she once carried me through
Her smile was evident in all that I'd do
She is no longer in my room

Laughter - she once kept my energy light
Her resounding voice filled the dark night
She is no longer in my room

Hope - she wove the way to a brighter day
Her promise kept me believing this was not the only way
She is no longer in my room

Confidence - she made me believe I was enough
Her "yes you can" was always just the right shove
She is no longer in my room

Song - she brought the wind to my words
Her notes of life carried them away on wingless birds
She is no longer in my room

Trust - she was my core to all that could be
Her life line unbreakable until it hit me
She is no longer in my room

Love - she was the greatest of them all
Her strength and compassion was my breaker of walls
She is no longer in my room

Anger - she came with a vengeance, pulled me into a deep trance
Sadness - she followed happily along, poking fun at my lost song
Fear - she hovered and made me forget, all that I hadn't done yet

Exhaustion - she ripped open my core, filled it with hate that I'd
    never known before
Hate - she lingered for a moment or two, swallowing my yellow
    and turning it blue... until
Numbness slowly crawled in to consume, all that was left of me in
    my room

I am not me anymore.

What Happened
by K. Christy Moore

What happened between what will be
And what is
A change of a universe
Lost dreams, lost loves, lost selves
Put away in the drawers of adulthood
Can they be taken out again
Shaken out, dusted off, altered to fit the new you?
Will they fit again, have they become moth-eaten
Or must we now shop for those who are new?

Haven of Strength
by Alison Romero

Spiralling down to an endless trench of darkness, engulfed with
    confusion, disparity and dismay
Struggling to break free of this self-destructive and emotional
    bondage
I reach desperately, with a grain of hope, to find me
Tormented with this addiction, like a drug, which impairs my
    sanity
An insatiable dire necessity to quench the savory of its poisonous
    nectar
As if, without it, leaves me deprived of air

I am horrendously petrified; for this is the normalcy I've known
    my entire life
Of being stripped of my self-worth, dignity and to be subservient
Living in a world of absolute absurdity
For I have never stood up to anyone; not even for me

I ponder relentlessly, in searching for an antidote to cure this
    infallible toxicity
I sought counseling, and absorbed knowledge of this
    treacherousness
And come to terms and acceptance of its vicious nature and my
    slow demise
My haven of protection and breakthrough lies dormant within
I must trust my instincts, hold on steadfast in faith, and partner
    with inner strength
Be courageous in endeavors of endless possibilities
And avow the truth that I am worthy, I am deserving

Although the answer seems so simple, so basic
It is the most exasperating, challenging battle to partake with one's
    self
Never looking back to see the bitterness, turmoil and wounds
Instead, victoriously embracing it, as an awakening.

Never Again

A Thousand Deaths
by Alison Romero

A moment of insatiable bliss
Leading only to Satan's abyss
Your infinite adoration above all
Succumbing to my inevitable fall

Entranced by your hypnotic appeal
A thief in the dark, my heart you steal
No escaping your alluring seduction
Bearing the gutted wounds of your destruction

I died a thousand deaths of heartaches
The solidity of my soul breaks
By the sharp, rusted blade of your thrusting words
In tiny, fragmented potteries of shards

A gentle hand you extend to me
You soothe the pain and we both agree
I weep in denial of unhappiness
Blame and cause was for only me to confess

And as I healed from these tortured pains
To ignite the fire of your gains
You poured acid, reopening wounds and bled
There were no more tears of fear I could shed

Years repeatedly endured the same
As I couldn't take your wretched game
So I gathered the strength and proceeded on
Behold, at last, love and hope
For you are gone.

Things Changed Forever, That Night
by Sally Olewe-Richards

Things changed forever, that night I stopped the madness
For one brief moment, and asked,
"You do know, don't you, that you'll never break me?"

After three years of you systematically trying to break me
Down to my very core
I still found the strength to finally leave

And with your final, last ditch
Desperate attempt to publicly humiliate me
You unwittingly handed me my power back
And set me free

With that, it stopped and I drew a line for good
Reclaiming my life back at the age of thirty three
Seeking a way to heal
From the years of pain and damage in the name of love!

Things changed forever, that night I stopped the madness
For one brief moment, and asked,
"You do know, don't you, that you'll never break me?"

Rapid-firing words to belittle, ridicule, demean
Over and over, incessant, never ending barrage of attacks
To make me feel like an absolute nobody
Again and again that I'm mentally ill
No one else likes me, only you can help me - love me!
A campaign to discredit me first to anyone I might cry out to for
  help

And with your final, last ditch
Desperate attempt to publicly humiliate me
You unwittingly handed me my power back
And set me free

The nasty slaps and spiteful kicks
Hot cigarette ash flicked in contempt
Pulling my finger back and watching it swell three times the size
All with a sense of glee
"If you could just be nice to me, these things wouldn't happen"
I would hear as I wept and sobbed, on repeat, ad nauseum
Into the long, dark, lonely nights

Things changed forever, that night I stopped the madness
For one brief moment, and asked,
"You do know, don't you, that you'll never break me?"

Damned if I do and damned if I don't, whatever I say is wrong
I'm always at fault - the one thing I can guarantee,
In one breath, both a selfish bitch
Inviting you to come out when you're tired from work
A lying cunt not wanting you there
If I then say 'Baby, stay home and rest'

And with your final, last ditch
Desperate attempt to publicly humiliate me
You unwittingly handed me my power back
And set me free

From loving you so completely
Blindly at whatever cost
To calmly standing by
And watching the last falling pieces of debris
Standing on the remains
Of a broken, poisonous love story
Unmoved by your latest empty-promise, sweet-talking plea

Things changed forever, that night I stopped the madness
For one brief moment, and asked,
"You do know, don't you, that you'll never break me?"

And with your final, last ditch
Desperate attempt to publicly humiliate me
You unwittingly handed me my power back
And set me free.

Blue Ribbon
by Cara Wiseman

Anyone would think
I'm addicted
To the pain I've
Been afflicted
A punishment
Upon myself
Whilst dust is
Collecting on the shelf
A ribbon fades
Losing its blue
I think less and
Less of you.

Peace to My Shore
by Debra Webster

The sea hits the rocks
Like your words on my heart
As the cold seeps right in
And turns my world dark

But just like the rocks
The cracks start to show
And though the light glimmers
It builds to a glow

The golden light rises
Bringing peace to my shore
Warming and healing
I know I'm worth more.

Ceily Lazore: "This is a photograph of one of my first handmade decorations for my bathroom. My gateway out of my depression is to try to create my own beauty that I can get lost in"

Where Is She, That Little Girl So Fragile and Free?
by Megan Hill

Where is she, that little girl so fragile and free?
Eyes big and bold
Innocence in her eyes
She could not be told

Where is she, that little girl so fragile and free?
She is long gone, wrapped in a world of hurt and pain
But to him it was all one big game
That game started slow with what seemed such little aim
But with every wrong move came consequence and blame
If only she could see it was all part of the game

Where is she, that little girl so fragile and free?
The game began when you conquered her body then mastered her
    mind
Her insecurities became your biggest find
By calling her ugly and fat
She believed that was a fact
If only she could see it was all part of the game

Where is she, that little girl so fragile and free?
She got to the next level of the game, all about control and power
He perfected his movements so she would always cower
With every raised voice he gave her a choice
What would you like now my love?
My fist or not to exist?
If only she could see it was all part of the game

Where is she, that little girl so fragile and free?
The next level of the game came with a slap or a punch
Shortly followed by a make-up lunch
That means he must love she
After-all, he knew her down to a tee
If only she could see it was all part of the game

Where is she, that little girl so fragile and free?
With no one to turn to
That was your cue
Bruise after bruise
You had nothing left to lose
If only she could see it was all part of the game

Where is she, that little girl so fragile and free?
You began to pull out her hair
And it ended in more than she could bear
Burning her legs with cigarettes
You weren't even left with any regrets
If only she could see it was all part of the game

Where is she, that little girl so fragile and free?
She has nothing left to give
As you whack her for the last time with the kitchen sieve
She was leaving the game broken and destroyed
Of course, that left you overjoyed
If only she could see it was all part of the game

Where is she, that little girl so fragile and free?
She has reached the end of the game wanting to die
Until that girl realised this was all a lie
You wanted to break her, destroy her and belittle her
And that is when she realised the aim of the game

Where is she, that little girl so fragile and free?
She loved you so deeply with nothing to gain
All you gave her was heartache and pain
You wanted to break that young girl so badly that she wanted to
    die
But unfortunately for you that game ended and she survived

Where is she, that young girl so fragile and free?
That young girl is me
I am Megan, not "psycho" or "she"
Now we have come to the end of the game
I am Megan so strong and free
The winner of the game is not you, it's me.

To My Future Me
by Tricia Merten

To my future me
Soon you will see
You haven't really lost your way

To the parts of me I lost
It wasn't at a cost
But you're better and stronger than yesterday

Your smile will get brighter
Your fears will seem lighter
You'll be able to say what you need to say

This too shall pass
It won't be just a mask
You are really going to be okay.

Just a Dream
by Skye

You seemed all that was
All that could be
I vanished slowly and faded with all that l could be
I thought it was me
For years on deaf ears
No remorse and only slight crocodile tears
My child is very sacred to my heart
Not a tool, a weapon or security guard
So go and plunder away from me
Leave us together and let us be
This game is no fun, we just want out
We ran away from your smoking gun
It may have appeared quiet, it may have been silent
But the screaming was loud and we are defiant!

No Contact
by Kim Alexandra

You see me now
With your unwelcome gaze
I've shut you out but you can't stop
I know your fury at my happiness
How much I've changed and healed
To be the woman I've become
Yet you just can't let me go
Can't let my life unfold
Without your grasp around me

But that's the thing you just don't see
You never truly had a hold over me
It was me who chose you
Forgave in you so much
Shows more about me
More than it does about you
Without you I stand proud
So much stronger, still nice
My heart always kind
But never fooled twice.

Rebirth
by Jo Moore

I feel my rage
Razors beneath my skin
Wanting to burst out
But I implode

Crushed concrete between my teeth
Burned rubber smell of my legs
The memory of butterflies stamped underfoot

You cannot take my eyes
That see beauty
Small shufflings towards the light

In the cellar of my mind
Encased in concrete
Frozen and lifeless
A spark ignites

Rebellion, anger
The overriding defiance
Has shaped me
Moulded me into fire

And I love
I burn.

Worth the Fight
by K. Christy Moore

I will not apologize for loving deeply
For expecting the best in everyone
For loving often

It is my heart that pays the price
Not yours
But I will never love again
Someone who doesn't love themselves
Who can't stand their own company
The quiet of their breath

I am capable of much
But I am no wizard
I am tired of working so hard
To convince you to stay
Either you know I am worth the effort
Or leave

If convincing is what you need
I am not what you are looking for.

Journey
by Solstice Rain Moon

I'm on my knees again; sometimes...
Sometimes
I wonder if it will be for eternities
I stand, I stagger, only to fall again
Your words, they echo
Sear like welts across my soul
They are like whispers in the dark; heavy
Telling me to quit; Whispers...
You, you are worthless
Not worth love, not worth me
Come back, I love you, I'm sorry...
Tears... more tearing at my soul

I gasp for air... no air comes
Will I pull through this time; this time I don't know
I feel the ripping, the ache so deep
I've crawled, dug my hands into the Earth
Felt Her tears rain down upon me, washing me as my own
Penetrating me
Pulling me out; I grasp for Her, crying out ...
She cradles me, as the Mother I never felt around me
I collapse, sobbing, raw ...
I let go
Go?
Where will I go...
I don't feel belonging anywhere

I want to; I thought that belonging was you, you and me
'Til forever, right?
But no. No! Don't go there anymore
I'm not your game, your supply ...
I was
But now I'm not
I've looked in your eyes, hopeful; always hopeful

To see that hope met with the depth that is in my soul...
Sometimes... sometimes I think that the depth I see is my own
Most times I don't
I question, always question
Such a spiral, these questions... will I ever find the answers
Then you call; you always call at the right time... for exactly the
    wrong reason
I'm cold... why am I so cold?

I'm shaking when I awake this time
The light is so bright, but it hurts...
I cry out
But wait... Don't leave me yet, I'm sorry
Why am I sorry?
Shhhhh... She cradles me... I sob

Love?
What is this? Who am I?
Do I exist? Maybe?
Could I?
I grasp for Her; for HER... I want her
She is beautiful, I know; she needs me
And I? I don't need him, I don't need them
I lift my face and I sigh; I sigh and I feel release
I fly upon the fear I once shied from, for I know
I know that I am a warrior
That my brokenness is my Rising
My Rising is my Awakening
My Awakening is my Re-birth
I feel the power of my wings thrusting me
My head is above water, my lungs deep within me
Full of Spirit, Truth, and Release
I
Will
Fucking
Be
Free.

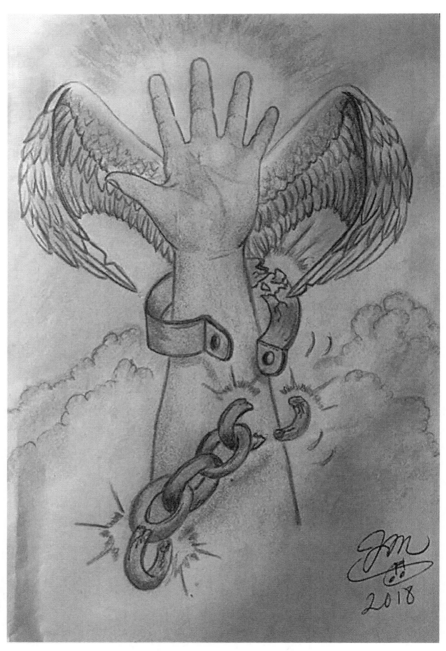

Jenney Moore: 'End of Oppression'

Never Again
by Alex Martin

I will never again be interpreted by others' insecurities
I will always aim to go further within and
Heal those places that attracted them
To begin with

I will never apologise or hide my light to
Placate another's demands to only share it
Solely with them
Whilst they parade around
Giving far-fetched love notes to anyone who
Appeases their ego

I will not ask permission to exist out loud.

Slipping Away
by Rachael Norcup

I was a rock in a stream
I sat peacefully
Content in the sun as time
Swept the world gently by
I didn't notice you creep up on me
Silently
I let you
I didn't struggle
I didn't think I needed to try

The stream I was in became your river
No land to steady my gaze
But still I thought I sat there safely
A rock to your river
But in truth I was slowly
Lost to your haze

As the days wore on I had faith
That my strength was my safety
Even as your river was rising
So the world's beauty slowly receded
The happiness I had was lost to me
Lost in the overbearing
Weight of your needs

Your smothering embrace engulfing me
I was buried in your depth and your noise
I didn't notice it
It happened so stealthily
Until one day
You had completely stifled my voice
I became one with your river

So I stayed there
Silently drowning
Believing the rush of your words
I thought through your roar
You had heard me
A deception in chaos
Used only to tighten your cords

You changed on a whim and with impunity
As seasons change so did you
Your summer was a
False sense of security
Because your winter
Always came back too

My strength I had believed in
And counted on
Like Ozymandias
I was a fool and it was gone

I was a rock no more
Just a pebble
My foundations
Their destruction complete
Swept away and dragged
By your current
A bedrock of sand
All that remained beneath my feet

But still I was a pebble
A part of myself was still there
No matter how much
You wore and chipped away at me
My soul was my own
Impossible for your abuse
To flay bare

I know that you thought
That you loved me
But your love was for you
Not for me
So I took what I saved
And I left you
Before your madness
Swept me away out to sea

Everything you took
Every hope you stole
Every smile you battered and bruised
None of these things could you possibly keep
I recovered them all when I left you
And not a tear for you
Shall I weep.

Monster
by MLB

It's over; you're a monster, I've seen you in the light
It's over; you're a monster, please just go without a fight
You've surely underestimated the black within my heart
By judging my demeanour right from the very start

I am not an easy target, not a pawn that you can play
I will not be a victim in your sadistic game
You cannot fault my honesty or the way I do portray
Who am I inside of me, it's how I will remain

That doesn't give you credence to treat me like a fool
I deserve the same respect that I would show to you
But a monster has no conscience or compass to guide his way
He is a fake illusion dressed in his tough and careless ways

No caring does he take for the chaos he did make
Instead he leaves abruptly with all that he can take
Needing you and I to feed him, keeping him awake
Without us he is empty, no feelings can he make

He is empty on the inside and tries to feed his soul
With the energy of others that he so cruelly stole
But if you deny him access to the passage of your heart
We can surely stop the monster's reign before it even starts.

The Journey
by Freedmum

"I rise" claims the Angel Maya
"He is risen" the congregation joyfully cry on Easter Sunday
I do not rise at all

I scramble my way through the darkness
Where the light flickers away in the distance
So far out of reach beyond my arm's length
A lifetime away
Clawing my way, fingertip by fingertip
From the bottomless pit where you threw me
Abandoning me to the crows
Who swoop and screech at me
Sweeping down to scrape out my eyes
Blurring the path and blocking the light

I tiptoe past the sleeping rats
Huddled together protecting each other
Their tails limp in slumber
How I wish I could rest my weary body
And close my tired eyes
But sleep never comes

When I close my eyes all I see
Is the taunting and sneering look on your face
I roll over to block out the sight
But all I hear are your condescending and bitter words
Tormenting me through the inky darkness
My eyes open to a fresh day
But I still don't rise
Picking my way slowly through
Along the path
Treading each step gently so as not to disturb
The dormant demons concealed in the shadows

Climbing over the jagged rocks
And sliding gently across smooth stones
The light fades again and the ceiling drops away
I drop to the floor and caterpillar my way through the indigo light

Exhaustion overtakes me and I drop to the ground
My legs no longer able to work
My breath returns, having held it for so long
Not to disturb the scavenging magpies
Desperate for their shining treasure
Tears sting my eyes

The dawn breaks with a muted sky
As the rain patters down against the path
Leaving the shimmering drops forming a glittering river
Snaking down the road
Suddenly the storm falters, the raging waves crash away
And a calm channel appears
Defining a bright clear path ahead
A trail to blaze my way into the light
A shining avenue, a passageway of dreams
Just opening up in front of my eyes

I round the corner and it appears
Guiding the way just as the Star of Bethlehem
It's there, just waiting for me to reach out
And grasp it with both hands
Tentatively I extend my hand, making gradual contact
I lunge towards it, claiming for my own
Taking it in arms, I tenderly caress
And hold it so tightly, never to be released again

I have claimed my prize, it's mine to hold and keep safe forever
Never to be stolen from me again
My body envelops my prize, drinking it in
Letting it permeate every pore and follicle
Never to seep away again
All the battles fought and victories claimed are mine alone
To taste and savour the sweetness of success
Never will I tread that path again
I am liberated
All my debts are discharged

And the Valley of Freedom beckons to me
The journey through the valley is just beginning
A new life to be filled with doubts and fears
A different path to be trod, filled with anticipation and expectation
Every morning dawns with a fresh challenge
To discover my way through the blooms and buds
That appear daily

The valley holds me close, not letting me stray
Allowing me to grow and nurture my prize
Filling me with hope and happiness
Encouraging me to learn and grow

This most novel journey of my life
Gives me the strength to smile and laugh
Trust and believe in the power
Of friendship and love.

Above All Else: Integrity
by Alex Martin

Above selfish desires and unmet wants: Integrity
Above fairytale stories and picket-fenced families: Integrity
Above egoic flattery and mass followings: Integrity
Above being proud and shifting honesty to the side: Integrity
Above losing recognition: Integrity
Above seeking fame at others' emotional expense: Integrity
Above pointless causes of unnecessary stress and worry: Integrity
Above playing the 'Game': Integrity
Above all else: Integrity.

I Know
by Villy Tentoma Zervou

You told me who I am
You told me what I need
You told me what I want
You told me what I can do
You told me you know better than me
And you only want the best for me

I trusted you
I believed you
I forgot who I really am
I forgot what I really want
I forgot what I really can do

But
A tiny piece of myself has never forgotten
You tried to kill this tiny piece but it was impossible
It just grew
And grew
And grew
Silently
Quietly
Slowly

And
I know who I am
I know what I need
I know what I want
I know what I can do

You are just not part of any of it.

Deconstruction
by Michelle N. Opel

The breaking
The unmaking
Rubble all around
Sitting amongst the bricks of broken dreams
Dust of destroyed hopes
Piles of pretending and pain
Masquerading as love

Trying to make sense
Any sense of it all
Sifting through the "what-ifs"
The "could've beens"
The "never will bes"
Running my hands through
The brokenness all around
It slips through my fingers
Out of my grasp

Amidst the rubble I see
The tiniest whisper of green
The smallest sprout of life
The precious bud of promise
Pushing through to the light
To the Light
And He reminds me to
Look up
Always look up.

And Here, I Will Fly

Debra Webster: 'Stepping into the Light'

Healing
by Alex Martin

Releasing what you built your reality upon
Letting go of stories, you so deeply wanted to believe in
Coming to terms that some humans cause injuries to others
Through a complex web of illusions
Designed to keep you stuck
For their fuel

Knowing you were played
Accepting the parts of me that made me prime bait
And played out my own trauma

Healing and releasing
Healing and releasing
One moment
One day at a time

I am dying a death of self that held me under
Numb and afraid
The shedding is at times uncomfortable
If not agony
But I see through the death, a light glinting
New and eager

I will honour this process
Every
Stage.

The Phoenix
by Kirsty Hutchinson

She's lived her whole life
But never been seen
When she looked in the mirror
Oh, who could she have been?
What would SHE like, instead of HE?

Done cowering in corners
Finished hanging her head
No longer a puppet
Who lays down and begs

The scars are healing
Though emotions run deep
The wounds now are closing
And she's finding her feet

The future in front
Looks shiny and new
She's now found her voice
All hers and all true

The waves no longer crashing
She has turned the tide
Her head now held high
And a spring in her stride

The pain she once felt
Now is fuelling her strength
She's strong now ... determined
And much more ... she's independent.

Goodbye
by Freedmum

You left but you didn't quite take everything away
You forgot to take the demon with you, just leaving it festering
    inside of me!

You took my soul, my dignity, my self-respect
Replacing them with your gremlins
Leaving them to grow inside me, eating away at me
They chomped away at my confidence, ripping away my smile
Crawling through my veins, creeping under my skin

Don't flatter yourself; the seeds were already there
You just inseminated them, feeding them daily
So they grew inside me, filling me with pain and fear
Pushing me, crushing me, filling every gap with pain

Your hard eyes fed the demon, filling every space within me
His hands scratched away inside me, his feet kicking me down
Your harsh words so vile, the gremlins laughed inside me
Echoing inside me, day in, day out

Your scornful jeers, such juicy fruit for the demon
He feasted upon them, savouring every juicy mouthful
The hateful sneers that scorched and burned my insides
Fuelling the fire for the demon's feast
Humiliation was spread through my veins, pumping around my
    body
Through every limb, every organ and seeping out through my skin
Your taunts and tantrums just dealt out so sweetly
The demon lapped them up, smacking his lips joyfully

The demon, the gremlins, they relished every name
You filled their hunger, making them greedier every day
Pain had so many strands reaching through my body
Digging through my heart, deep into my soul

Daily they gorged on the feast you fed
Gluttonous obesity keeping them gratified
As with every living thing, they need nourishment to survive
Hydration to thrive
But you abandoned them to starve

The first few weeks, they were so full, so fat
They didn't miss their daily intake of taunts and tears
But soon they noticed that you had gone
With no fresh jibes to feed them
Left with only memories for their sustenance
But echoes didn't placate them

They pushed and fought inside me, waiting to be fed
They waited, tummies rumbling
But not even a crumb was thrown their way
They screamed and yelled, pushing and shoving each other
Kicking and brawling
But not even a scrap was thrown their way

Like baby chicks crying for their mother
You left them abandoned in the nest

But then along came the cuckoo, pushing in its way
Planting itself to feast on new food
The cuckoo grew on smiles, soft words helped it along
With every happy thought a gremlin was gone

Anger was the first one, reluctantly dragging his feet
A homeless gremlin looking for a new space to invade
Fear was off like a shot, departing with a flounce
Off to find a new home, to feed on someone else's misery

Shame soon became homeless, seeking pastures new
Joy and Enthusiasm began to work their way through
Humiliation dragged his heels, but along came Self-Respect
Kicking his butt all the way to a new home

Confidence came next, shoving its way in
Barging his way to fill the gap left by Rage
These forgotten feelings, hidden so long
Now fill me with the things I lost

Happiness, so missed, fills my soul, my being
It shows through the smile I wear
My head held high, shiny bright eyes
Never to be replaced
My smile is staying there.

Rain Water Music
by Suzanne Sandstrom

Rain water music
On the railing
The bell and the whistle and the sea;
Song of a change
Sounds of a clearing of the air
I breathe
All that who have been smothered
Breathe
Clean and crisp and new
The revival of a life starved
For freshness too long
I breathe in hard
The clear.

Who Am I After It All?
by Cara Wiseman

The brain can't fathom what the heart can't see
The soul can't inhibit all that one can be
When you look inside and know it's she
The person I'm meant to be is me.

Heartbreak
by Emma Hall

Heartbreak can be the best thing that can happen to you
In the hardest way.
But the start of a breakup feels more like betray
Maybe your ex was led astray

The grief hits you like a wave
You are shocked and in denial
There is nothing that anyone can do or say
People will gather round to hear
The unhappy song you sing
But scatter to the wind
They go when broken records begin to ring

You are left alone to find your way
You travel alone as you struggle
To get through another day.
You look down at your phone
And yet another empty inbox is on display

"How can heartbreak be the best thing
That happens to us the hardest way?" I hear you say
My love, you will find out in time
When your true soulmate comes
One day.

The Pain
by Kimberly R. Hudson, Ed.D

The pain of a love you thought was real
Takes days, months, years to heal

The lies, the deceit, the cheating
Showed this love had no meaning

The pain of love lost
You figure your way through
You must
You have children depending on you

You drink, you pray, you eat, you sleep
You fight through the pain to find some peace

It can be done, it's been done before
To risk going through the pain, once more

You lose yourself, your mind with a Narc
You forget how to live
How to be productive
How to start

You lose yourself and you don't care
Because you seek a love
That was never really there

It will be OK, I know it for sure
The pain is now gone
This new love is pure

No more pain of lost love
No more deception or lies
Just pure love and joy
And happiness now resides.

Ann Clayton-Murray: 'A journey for a beautiful life of peace within'

The Shack
by Natalia García

Walking through the forest, a woman notices a shack in the
    distance
She's tired and exhausted from a long journey
She hasn't stopped for a long time
Carrying a lot of weight on her back
And she decides it's time to rest

As she gets closer to the shack, she knocks at the door
But nobody answers
She knocks again and the door suddenly opens
But there's no one there
She decides to walk in and everything looks so different from the
    outside
It's a very cold and big room
The room is dirty, empty, and dark
All of a sudden, she notices she has company
But for some reason she is not scared

She sees this little girl in a corner, sitting on the floor
She looks dirty, wounded, and very scared
In a strange and almost impossible way, the woman starts to see in
    her heart
How the little girl feels

She's in fear, hopeless, disappointed, and beaten
Her heart has been shattered in a thousand pieces
She has been touched, not in a nice way
Not in an allowed way
Her dreams are torn and trampled
She is about to give up
She feels so lost that she thinks the only way to escape her pain is
    death
There is no more fight in her
"I've got to help her", the woman thinks!

As she slowly walks towards that corner, the little girl looks at the
    woman
She thinks she's the most beautiful woman she's ever seen
That woman is strong and she feels the love and kindness in her
    heart
She knows she's not going to hurt her

The woman kneels in front of her and carefully
Extending her hand and without saying a word
Invites the little girl to get up
Tears starts to roll down her little face but she starts to feel safe
She knows she can trust this woman and slowly gets up
The woman wipes her tears and smiles while saying
"Everything is going to be OK sweetheart, come with me..."

The little girl hesitates for a second
But after taking a deep breath
She embraces that little drop of hope and braveness inside her
And slowly regains strength to get up

They head towards the door, holding hands
When the woman opens the door
After a long time of being in that horrible shack
The little girl finally sees the sunlight

In front of them there is a beautiful and colourful field
The sunlight kisses her skin
And the warmth makes this little girl feel stronger
And stronger
She's no longer afraid

"I understand your pain better than anybody else
I know what you've been through
And I'm really sorry I could not prevent it
I'm so sorry I couldn't protect you before
But I promise you this
From this point forward, your life will be different

Everything that you deserve in life will come to you
Your heart will heal and the darkness will turn into light
Your dreams will come true
And nothing but happiness will fill your soul", the woman says
A beautiful smile is drawn on her face as she stares at the woman

They hug and get lost in that beautiful moment
Then suddenly the little girl starts to vanish into the air
Her spirit merges with the wind, dancing with the flowers
Rising to the sky
She is free, finally free!!!

The woman, with great astonishment
Observes what happens in front of her eyes
Nostalgia invades her heart as to her surprise
She realizes that little girl was her all this time

She conquered her fears
She decided to be brave
She fought hard to let go of the things
That kept her heart in that dark place
For so long
She defeated her enemies
She's victorious
And that woman... is me.

Inner Sense
by Charlotte Mather

Lottie is the child who tiptoes in my soul
She is brave and kind and happy
The piece that makes me whole
Lottie lives a life worth living though she's only 6 years old
She dances like she has no worries
Lottie shines like gold

When I find myself unstuck and breaking at my seams
Lottie fetches craft glue and stitches me with dreams
Darkness cannot touch me with Lottie by my side
She blows raspberries at my demons, Lottie doesn't hide
Lottie tells me that she loves me, a hundred times a day
And when I'm lost in hopelessness, Lottie guides my way.

Phoenix Rising
by Kim Alexandra

You had never felt that way before, we were true soulmates
A once in a lifetime real romance, nothing else came close

You spoke to me through lies and veils, you promised me it all
I trusted what you said to me, I'd not met one like you before

Your deceit was whole, complete and wild
Your charm played through my soul

You set me up, plunged through my mind, you harvested my
    dreams
Nothing of me was left alone, you raged, you took, you stole

You held my trust and once you did, you played to shut us down
Not once, or twice but many times, the trauma bond complete

You left me bare, exposed and spent
But this farce you did not win

Through it all you misjudged me, I'm tougher than you thought
I am stronger now despite your games, I am once more whole.

Kate Sanderson: "This is a photograph of a piece of glass art that I created to symbolise soaring hope and renewal. It then accidentally cracked through due to stress on the glass. It shows the scars of its journey, but then when allowed to bask in the light, it becomes transfigured into something truly wonderful, imperfections and all. I think it makes a nice metaphor for the journey that survivors go through."

PART TWO: And Here, I Will Fly
by Yvette Bruni

What happened to the person that stood before me?
Well, here I am
Testimony to my former self
The person who laughed at life
And loved the days
The girl who used to sing at the top of her voice
And didn't care who heard
I was her and here she is now
I stood for so long, a butterfly with broken wings

I don't want a life like that anymore
I had to shout it from the rooftops
But I couldn't find my voice
Which was buried deep within me
Where are you, voice?
Where is my courage to make a stand?

Fragility deep down
Held my heart in place
And chaos ruled my world
You see I grew used to this life
It shouldn't have been that way
My heart ruled my head

Self -blame I wore as a badge of honour
Did I create all this mess and destruction?
I grew to doubt myself
And you transferred the blame at my door
You did it so well, it was your craft

I'm not saying it was all one sided
I'm not going to write these words
And make them all about you
You are not my narrative
And my narrative shall not be taken by you
You pale to insignificance

So what happened?
My wings managed to repair themselves
It was not easy
Felt like a lifetime
To put them back together again

All the years had now rolled into one day
I've been blinded
Not by the truth
But by taking my life back
I wanted it back so much
I could feel, taste and smell it

And now, here I stand in a place of tranquillity
I can hear you now
But I'm not going to invite the chaos in
The hands that threw me a lifeline
Have now guided me back

This time I will wear the words of wisdom
Like a suit of armour that will never
Be penetrated or broken down
I played my part
But I had to find the truth
which slowly uncovered
And showed itself to me

Here I now stand
Not a shadow of my former self
But the real me
Courageous and strong
A sense of sadness falls over me
But it doesn't last long

I've been given
A second chance at life
I'm not going to recite
The old clichés
Not going to lay
Any kind of blame

But one thing I will say:
I will never let my wings
Be broken again.

A Message for my Queens
by Christelle Rodriguez

Hey Queen
Yes you!
Hold your head up high
Love yourself the way you deserve to be loved
Get up out of that DARKNESS
Find your way into the LIGHT

You have a PURPOSE in this life
You matter
You are loved by many

Stand up and let me help you straighten that crown, Queen
Because the truth of the matter is
REAL QUEENS ALWAYS UPLIFT OTHER QUEENS.

Peace to all of you beautiful souls
Namaste
#kreethequeenmotivator

11:11, Letting Go
by Tina M. Durbin

On this night, I write
The next chapter of a book I lived
And pages I turned
Along with memories I burned

Survivors often live in a state of fight or flight
We are fighting so hard in so many ways
For so many reasons
That we aren't sure at times
What we are even fighting for
Some days

We fight for peace
We fight for understanding
We fight for illusions
We fight for sanity
We fight for what we want
We fight for voice

In flight we also fight
We fight for peace through silence
We fight for understanding through knowledge
We fight for illusions that seemed like a reality
We fight for sanity as we process
We fight for voice with screams and silence

At the end of day
We fight for the flight to let go
We let go of blame
We let go of shame
We let go of illusions
We let go of confusion
We let go of chaos
We let go of trauma

We let go of tears
We let go of anxiety
We let go of fear
We let go of change

Ah ... we simply (over time) let go

Letting go is the culmination of FIGHT and FLIGHT
Tonight I am letting go of a fight
To save a reality that never existed
Tonight I let go of confusion
That was nothing more than chaos and confusion
Twisted

If I can tell you anything
About the process of becoming a survivor
Know this one thing
The reality of the illusion
Is the game
And the illusion of the reality
Is not your blame
Or shame
Let go of the emotional games of your abuser
And work to foster a love of self
Far greater than any love known on earth
Let an inner guide help to find
The YOU that exists
Among all the twists
Of a reality YOU will create
For yourself

Survivors survive
Survivors thrive

Survivors let go

Tonight
My fight and flight culminate
In letting go

In gratitude, 11:11.

The Air of Freedom
by Uchenna Nwigwe Nwosu-Igbo

Oh I loved him
The heck, I still do

I was brought up in Nigeria but by parents who had their lives in
'Western Germany'
So I can't be termed as a typical African with regards to my
upbringing, why?
I've always had a voice!
Mehn! Was I confused about patriarchy and being a wife in African
terms
I think to a large extent, there's still that struggle
So what did I do?

I've always been a chatterbox so I shared with the love of my life
at the time
I told him how a successful marriage was my first definition of life
success

Oh boy, was that a mistake

He threatened me with divorce every chance he got
Because during marriage counselling before the wedding, we were
warned against such threats
So he avoided the word and then it was "I don't think this is
working"
That statement scared the life out of me
Then I began to walk on eggshells
(Or that's when I noticed I was afraid)

There's no fear in love Uchenna, so how did you fear and still love?
I know not
I knew something was wrong with the relationship.
He knew too and kept saying "the foundation is wrong, you lied to
me"

Yes, I used to lie about insignificant things as I feared the outcome of the truth
And because I couldn't cope with the lies, I'd come out clean
And that would be filed to use against me in the near future
And accuse me of not being trustworthy

So many memories
One of his sisters said, "I'm happy my brother is marrying you, cos you're a strong woman'
Another said quite early in the marriage, "The grass is not greener outside so don't mind anyone deceiving you to leave your marriage"
That was shocking because I'd never imagined anything but death separating me from my spouse
It took me over eight years to realise they saw the signs
They could relate with a lot of things because he inherited it and as their only brother
I was a good cover up for the mess the family was

Oh I loved him
Or still do. Not a chance

I used to say, "You keep threatening me with a divorce, I'll never do that to you but you should be afraid if I ever take a walk"
Guess what?
I did take a walk one night in 2017 with our one year old daughter
I hoped the child would matter and he would ask for her.
I just wanted to have a reason to be with him even if it was the child
I needed one of us to be wanted and that would be something to hold onto

He rather wrote a letter and copied the police and my family
He claimed I left the house with my daughter and he didn't know where I went
My phone was on, he never dialled
He knew I'd be back

I had nothing financially
Twelve hours later, after calls from my dad, a close relative and then my pastor, we were back and the locks were changed
He had given an instruction that he had to be back first before I get in

So they shouldn't allow his crazy wife to break the locks

We stayed, I, like a dog with its tail between its legs and waited for
    him
And he came in like a god, opened the door and let us in
I'd never felt so unwanted until then and worse, I felt for my
    daughter

Three years down the line, pregnant again, he was verbally,
    physically and financially abusive. And that pregnancy
The child (ren) mattered to me and so I took a temporary walk
    with my 3 year old daughter at the time
Little did I know that I'd never go back

Oh I ran away from West Africa to protect my sanity and my
    children
To close my ears to religious/spiritual abuse
To close my ears to manipulation
To hold my feet from running back to him when I was tired of
    questions from the children
To secure the health of my unborn baby
Who was in danger from having things thrown at me while
    pregnant
Little did I know that my desire to have a better biological father
    for my children than a good husband
Wouldn't be met with him
But here I am
Ready to love and give and be me
And be free

I had been virtually banned from socializing with my good friends
Instructed to stay off Facebook
Pushed to hide, to shrink myself
And this "smartass chick" did
Oh I did

I had to be a 'submissive wife'
His definition of submission: obey without complaint, as far as I
    don't stop you from worshipping God
His words: "I want you to be a doormat, when I walk through the
    door, I won't step on you

But even if I do, I want you to be submissive enough to trust God
   to fight for you and deal with me"

I've been so confident all my life but at some point I was hiding
I didn't want to be heard
I've been particular about being seen but I liked to write, to talk
   and share

Now, I write again
I am free
I have no secrets, he's done well in sharing all I shared with him
I am FREE!

Carnival
by Valena

My life was a wild runaway train
A roller coaster with loose seat belts
Broken latches, squeaky wheels
Sparks flying from the tracks

A Tilt-a'Whirl
A hall of mirrors
Waking up in that spinning tube
You have to walk to exit

I had cotton candy fingers
And motorcycle hair

The horses I chose
Connected to carousels

The music made me sick

I crawled after running
Walked after standing
Began to fly
Came back to Earth
And now I stand.

Supernova
by Alex Martin

A supernova was born in her heart
It consumed her whole body so fast
That it created more stars in every cell
Galaxies formed on their journey
Through her veins
Sustained by her life force

Her light grew so powerful, gaining speed
Faster and faster so that she became
Her own gravitational pull
Black holes forming through the spaces
Of her breath

Her body became the canvas of a multiverse
Glistening beauty beyond the conceptions of the mind
She is God incarnate
Pure unconditional love
Divinity.

My Red Quilt
by K. Christy Moore

I took all the red flags he waved
And made a quilt for our bed
Crimson with the lies and mistruths
Green with jealousy I felt toward
The other women his attention was directed to

I stitched it with the threads of pain and tears
Adorned it with shards of my heart and broken promises
And I stuffed it with all my feelings so
I could remain numb under its weight

I lay still under my cover, cold and hopeful
Dreaming of what could, would, ever happen
If he changed
For him to see the power of my love
And heal himself

I buried my dreams under the nightmares
And grew strong
Powerful enough to rise again
A Phoenix
Seared and scorched, lessons learned.

Debra Webster: 'My Red Quilt'

Your Story

The Journey to Healing from Narcissistic Abuse

Healing from narcissistic abuse can be likened to that poignant scene from the film The Shawshank Redemption. The film tells the story of Andy Dufresne, wrongfully found guilty of a crime he didn't commit, then incarcerated in a hellhole prison for many years, where he endures horrific abuse at the hands of inmates and wardens. Eventually, he is able to escape, but to reach freedom he has to crawl through a half-mile long sewer, filled with stomach-turning filth, that leads from the prison to freedom. There's an iconic scene, where upon reaching the end of the sewer tunnel, Andy emerges triumphantly and raises his arms up to the sky, as heavy rain washes him clean. Later, we see he's succeeded in creating the life he always dreamed of, restoring boats on a beautiful, sunny beach in Mexico.

It's useful to understand that healing from narcissistic abuse is a similar process. After years in a hellhole prison with an abuser, to reach freedom, we have to wade through the internal sewers of our pain and trauma. The only way out is through this tunnel and at times it will feel terrifyingly oppressive and like there's never going to be an end. But as deeply unpleasant as it is, liberation is waiting on the other side. One day, we realise we can breathe properly again. We can close our eyes and feel the metaphorical, cleansing rain washing over us as we raise our arms up high, beaming and jubilant at our new-found freedom. It's following this emancipation, that we can truly create the life we deserve.

The sewer, in this case, is the process of allowing ourselves to sit with, feel, work through and ultimately release years of pain and suffering. We may find the wounds we need to heal run very deep (perhaps even back to childhood) but allowing them to be seen, heard and honoured will make it possible to let them go and move forwards to a brighter, happier future.

The Power of Writing Your Story

A wonderful way to explore this healing inner work is through writing about your experiences and feelings. In fact, this type of expressive writing has been scientifically proven to have incredible benefits for healing from trauma.

The editors of this book have both used expressive writing, including journaling and poetry, as a healing tool at different points in their lives.

Stephanie, who's had a lifelong love of words, has found writing to be both a release and a comfort during times of loss and grief in her life. After her first pregnancy, 25 years ago, ended in a miscarriage at 13 weeks, she found she suppressed her emotions and never truly acknowledged the sense of loss and failure or allowed herself to grieve for what might have been. In recent years, almost without knowing it, the event has seeped into her poetry and allowed her to accept that it happened and that it hurt. By referring to it "aloud", she feels comforted that she can remember that potential child's existence and grieve its loss.

In the summer of 2020, her beloved mother passed away, which left Stephanie feeling numb and traumatised. Initially, thinking she was coping well but in reality using distractions to prevent herself from giving way to what felt like a terrifying burden of grief.

Like many of us, she has often buried uncomfortable emotions, intending to retrieve them later when she feels stronger. This is a

144

coping mechanism but if it goes on too long it can be hard to "unbury" the emotions in order to deal with them, and they can fester and make it harder to heal.

However, over a particular period of days in the later months of 2020, Stephanie felt the urge to write and two poems emerged. Although they weren't a literal account of her mother's death and how desolate she felt, they mentioned her, both overtly and subtly, as much as she could bear to. Just by committing her mother onto paper made her loss real. Stephanie could no longer deny the grief but had to open herself to the pain. This is an ongoing process and will continue for her, but she knows that her writing allows her to express agonising emotions in what feels like a safe and controlled way, and that in turn will help her to recover.

Sally has enjoyed writing since childhood and always found it to be both a comfort and an escape. During teenage years she was an ardent journaler, so returned to this after she left her abusive ex and decided to travel - literally - to put an ocean between them. The next 18 months turned into her own personal 'Eat, Pray, Love' experience - there may very well be another book there! - and although her journals had been purchased to record her travels, she inevitably ended up pouring over details of the relationship and trying to make sense of it.

It was several years later, when she came across an article in *Elephant Journal* by Alex Myles, titled 'The Toxic Attraction Between an Empath and a Narcissist' that the penny dropped that's what she had experienced. So, at the time of traveling and trying to break a trauma bond with no point of reference for what this toxic dynamic was, journaling was a way of releasing pain and trying to find her way through the madness to see the truth. Tear-stained pages talk about needing to 'break the cycle' with him, of 'getting sucked back into the relationship' and of her need 'to go no contact' to break free - with hindsight it makes fascinating reading. All of the struggles we have are there to see; wrestling with triangulation, the pain of missing a mirage that never truly was and seeking to control the only thing we ever can, her own responses to this situation. This journal was a silent 'therapist' that would listen without judgement, but by 'talking' through this outpouring on the page, it was possible to join the dots and make sense of things.

In fact, James Pennebaker, a University of Texas at Austin social psychologist and researcher, conducted some fascinating research in the early 1980s, to test the psychological impact of writing and the similarities between 'journal therapy' and 'talk therapy'. There is a significant and ever-growing body of research that shows expressive writing through journaling is an effective therapeutic tool to support healing from a range of emotional and physical responses to difficult experiences, including anxiety, addiction, grief, depression, stress and trauma.

It may sound counterintuitive to say that writing about painful experiences is therapeutic. However, by writing about it, we're *releasing* these memories and choosing to let go of the burden of carrying them around with us any longer. Writing down our thoughts and feelings gets them out of our heads and allows us to make sense of them. To understand clearly that we were never to blame for things we've been subjected to and any shame is misplaced.

"I found that writing was a great process for dealing with hidden trauma. Finding a way to 'let go' helps us to 'move on'."
- Mary Wride,
author of '*The Song of Truth*'

146

Pennebaker believes that writing about stressful and traumatic events helps us come to terms with them, which lowers the impact of these stressors on our physical health and can even strengthen immune cells!

In support of these findings, researchers Stephen Lepore and Joshua Smyth, authors of the book 'The Writing Cure: How Expressive Writing Promotes Health and Emotional Well-being', discovered that people who suffered deeply from an overwhelm of negative emotions and behaviours could use journaling as a means of managing, and even overcoming, those feelings. They found that this helped people to regulate their emotions as well as strengthening the immune system and helping to protect the body from disease. Additional studies have shown it can decrease the symptoms of asthma and rheumatoid arthritis. A 2013 study, carried out in New Zealand by Heidi E. Koschwanez et al., reported journaling helped in speeding up wound healing!

By working through recovery at our own pace, it enables us to profoundly reconnect with our thoughts and feelings. Together with other tools and recovery resources, writing about our experiences can become an outlet to releasing pain and finding the answers we seek. We have them inside of us and journaling helps to discover them by connecting back to our own deep knowing and wisdom. Over time we can begin to look back over past entries and see patterns emerging or perhaps even where we've made shifts and progress in our healing. We begin to break the narcissist's addictive spell - the trauma bond - when we reconnect back to the truth, to our own wisdom and power, and to one another through supportive communities.

The physical action of writing down our thoughts with pen to paper (or finger to keyboard) is a somatic process - connecting our body and mind - which can further aid our recovery. This mental and physical release of emotions, which are too heavy and painful to bear, brings relief and calm.

Let your voice be heard.

This can be either freeform/stream of consciousness writing, noting down everything that comes into our heads as we sit there, or it can be writing about a specific memory, feeling or thought we've had. If you would like a more structured approach to be guided through writing about your experiences, 'Woman in Progress: The Reflexive Journal For Women and Girls Subjected to Abuse and Trauma' by Dr Jessica Taylor (2020) is a wonderful resource.

Journaling can help us to make sense of our experiences and see through the fog of confusion the narcissist has created. At the start of our journey, we very well may be feeling we're somehow to blame for what's happened. We may wonder are we the narcissist? Often, it's hard to know up from down after the rollercoaster of emotions we've been subjected to throughout the relationship. By writing it all down, then re-reading our words and seeing it with fresh eyes, we can begin to see the truth more clearly.

What do we feel about this woman who's endured so much?

What do we want her to know?

You don't have to know what you're going to write when you start - just write.

"What a comfort is this journal I tell myself to myself and throw the burden on my book and feel relieved"
– Anne Lister

This book of our innermost thoughts, feelings, secrets, wishes and fears can become the trusted friend we confide in without worrying about boring them or feeling they might judge us. Remember, this is just for your eyes only.

Journaling is a perfect way to start writing therapeutically, but if you do feel inspired to write poetry, you can begin using your journal to experiment with this. It's a wonderful, creative way to unlock our thoughts and to be able to express a tsunami of emotions in a very precise way. This can be incredibly powerful and we explain more about how to start exploring writing poetry, in the next section.

> *"In very few words you can say powerful things. After Sally's encouragement, I tried to write a poem. I was quite impressed because it was all my feelings, but I put them into 10 lines!"*
> – Villy Tentoma Zervou

First things first, what actually *is* poetry?

Poetry has different meanings to different people – some people immediately think of the rhymes of their childhood days; others may think about limericks and other funny poems; while still others might think poetry is "arty", pretentious, hard to understand, not for "ordinary" people.

The truth is, it can be all those things and more, but when we are the writer, poetry is first and foremost a way of expressing ourselves creatively. We can write about events, people, beautiful places and strong emotions and we can use poetry to think about our place in the world, our experiences, our hopes and our dreams and to make sense of things that may have happened to us.

By now, you may have read many of the poems in the section *Her Story*, which so beautifully shows that poems can take many different forms and the most important thing is that they come from the heart.

What poetry is NOT!

It's time to bust some myths about poetry that can sometimes put people off from reading or writing it.

Poetry is boring It's not!! Or at least it doesn't have to be, as you will have seen from the poems in the *Her Story* section of this book. One of the biggest and most enjoyable challenges of writing descriptive poetry is finding new and interesting ways to describe objects, scenes and feelings. When the reader comes across a description that conjures up a vivid image in their mind or a phrase that describes something in a way that they had never imagined, it's like being struck by lightning – in a good way!

> *"I think it's a complete privilege to read a poem that somebody has written; it's almost like you're sharing their soul because it's written from very deep within."*
> – Hilary Daw

Poetry is pretentious and hard to understand It's not! Or at least it doesn't have to be. There is a perception that poets deliberately hide the meaning of their writing and make it difficult for ordinary people to understand, in order to appear "clever". While some poetry is undoubtedly hard to penetrate, poetry is so diverse that there really is something for everyone.

Poetry is really hard to write It really is not! If you are writing from the heart, if you are writing something that is beautiful or sad or amazing; something that moves you or is important to you, your passion will come across and your reader will feel that.

Poetry has to rhyme No it doesn't! It can if you want it to, but it doesn't have to. Many of the more "highbrow" modern poets are a bit snobby about rhyming poetry, but rhyme can really help with understanding the meaning, and many people prefer to listen to poetry that rhymes. Do bear in mind though, when writing poetry, a possible pitfall is that sometimes a word can be put in simply because it rhymes and it doesn't always add to the meaning of the poem. However, when you can find a word that rhymes and is exactly right to get your message across, that's when you get poetry magic!

Rhymes have to be at the ends of lines They often are but they don't have to be. Some rhymes can be internal where the rhyme is in the middle of the line. Some poems have a rhyme at the end of a line and then the rhyming word in the middle of the next line. It's completely up to you, so experiment with that and see what works.

Poems have to have a regular rhythm Many do, but they absolutely don't have to. However, there should be a natural flow that you will hear when you read it out, so listen carefully to see if you can hear it!

"I thought poetry always had to rhyme and have the same cadence and all the lines had to be the same length, and that isn't how it comes to me."
– K. Christy Moore

Poetic terms

Russian writer Anton Checkov said, *"Don't tell me the moon is shining, show me the glint of light on broken glass"* and this illustrates a key difference between poetry and other forms of writing. There are various terms and techniques used in poetry, which all help to identify it as poetry and help it to flow and sound right when listening to it, for example the musicality that's created through alliteration and assonance. Here are a few you could try experimenting with:

Alliteration Repeating words that start with the same letter or the same sound, for example "sparkling stars".

Assonance Repeating words that have the same vowel sounds, for example "deep green sea".

Consonance Repeating words that have the same consonant sounds in quick succession in a sentence, for example "grassy summer days".

Metaphor Using a non-related thing to describe another, for example describing a river as a "snake, slithering across the land".

Simile Describing one thing as another that is not obviously similar. Similar to metaphor but similes always use a word such as "like" or "as", for example "The moon is glowing like a silver coin".

"It can be an experience just to write and it's cathartic; it helps you to define yourself and your feelings. It's also a safe way to abstractly express yourself, if you're in a domestic violence situation, where they will not really understand what you're talking about anyway"
– Valena

Your poem, Your Story

Your poem can be funny or sad or somewhere in between – none of us is wholly one thing or another and the beauty of a poem is that it can reflect all sides of you. If you find you really enjoy this as a creative outlet, you might like to try using some of the poetic techniques mentioned, or even researching others you could use. Here are some ideas on the shape your poem might take to help you get started:

- Your poem might be in the form of a letter to someone who has harmed you, for example: Dear ... you may think I'm like this but really, who I am is this.
- It could be a series of repetitions of "I am" ... (strong, scared, brave, happy etc.) List all the things you have been and now are, or want to be. Think hard about every aspect of yourself.
- You could talk about a particular incident that had a profound effect on you. Did you realise something or change because of it?
- You may like to write a 'resonance' poem based on the title, themes or style of one of the poems which resonated with you in the *Her Story* section of the book.
- If you are in the process of becoming who you really are, say it! Affirm the dream "you" in your poem.

To begin with, don't overthink it; just relax and experiment with words, and be kind to yourself. This is your opportunity to connect more deeply back to yourself, so just see what arises and trust the process.

Above all, enjoy creating and be proud of yourself!

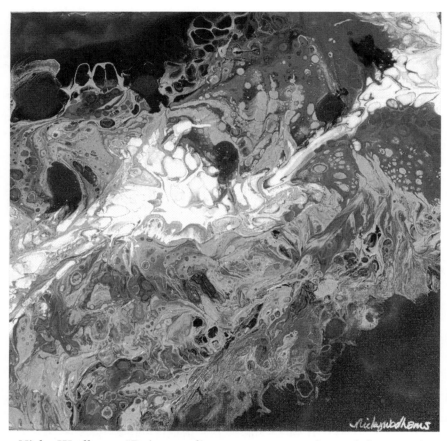

Nicky Wodhams: "Doing acrylic pours was a creative and therapeutic outlet for me after having spent 27 years with a narcissist. I'm two years out and very happy to be free. There's something satisfying about creating and not necessarily knowing what the outcome will be but being happy with that nonetheless."

Preparing to Write

Creating the right environment

The beauty of writing is that you need very little to start. All you really need is a pen and some paper or you may feel you prefer to type on your laptop for ease. The most important thing is just to write, so do whichever feels best for you. However, studies have shown that writing by hand activates more areas of the brain than writing on a computer.

The act of physically writing accesses your left brain, which is analytical and rational. While your left brain is busy focusing on the activity of writing, it allows your right brain the freedom to create and feel, which removes mental blocks and allows you to better understand yourself, others and the world around you.

As one of the main reasons for using expressive writing as a recovery resource is to unlock and examine the thoughts and feelings you're experiencing, it's best to do it with a pen and paper, if you can. However, do keep in mind securing your privacy. It may be safer to use your laptop or even an online app, which will store your notes and password protect them. If you prefer to write in a traditional journal, think about buying a lockbox to keep it in.

You're about to embark on a great journey to release yourself from pain and fear you may have been carrying around for years, so if you're going the traditional route, you may like to treat yourself to a special notebook to journal in, perhaps even a new pen or pencil.

The doing matters more than the tools, but who doesn't like a pretty notebook and pen! If you're going to pour your heart out, you may as well do it over pages encased in a cover that speaks to you and makes you want to open it and begin. For the same reason, finding a comfortable pen is also important. It can be any old Biro that's lying around really, but having a pen that you can easily glide over the pages as your mind comes to life on the page, will make the work much easier on your fingers.

Where possible, organise a space you can feel comfortable to write in and ensure you can have privacy while you write, so that you can just let go. Although you ideally want somewhere quiet, you may like to have some music playing softly in the background. It's best to turn off the TV, phone and other distractions though. You may like to light some scented candles to create a nice ambience.

If you are new to writing, you may find that the first sentence is the hardest to start. Begin anywhere, and forget spelling and punctuation. This is for your eyes only, so just write from the heart and see what comes out. Write quickly and try not to judge or censor yourself.

Revisiting the past, but returning safely to the present

When writing about your experiences, you will very likely find difficult emotions arise. You might even experience feelings of panic or overwhelm at the memories and feelings. It's important to look after yourself first and if you know that certain experiences have been particularly traumatising for you, you may want to speak to a counsellor or trusted friend, before working through them alone.

Try to add 10 minutes of post-writing time for you to collect yourself and your thoughts and return to the present moment. You may feel sad after writing or experience other strong emotions, so it's important to have a little time for reflection and to ground.

"It is normal for writing to feel cathartic and useful, but it is also normal for writing to feel stressful, triggering or exhausting. You may need to pace yourself... and take good care of your wellbeing whilst writing."
– Dr Jessica Taylor,
Woman In Progress.

Here's an often used, calming technique to reconnect back to your body and five senses, to help remind you that right now, in this moment, you're safe.

The 5, 4, 3, 2, 1 Grounding Technique

Take a deep belly breath to begin. Breathe in for the count of four and out for the count of six.

5 - LOOK: Look around for five things that you can see, and say them out loud. For example, you could say, I see the computer, I see the cup, I see the picture frame.

4 - FEEL: Pay attention to your body and think of four things that you can feel, and say them out loud. For example, you could say, I feel my feet warm in my socks, I feel the hair on the back of my neck, or I feel the pillow I am sitting on.

3 - LISTEN: Listen for three sounds. It could be the sound of traffic outside, the sound of typing or the sound of your tummy rumbling. Say the three things out loud.

2 - SMELL: Say two things you can smell. If you can't smell anything at the moment, then name your two favourite smells.

1 - TASTE: Say one thing you can taste. For example, it may be the toothpaste from brushing your teeth or the camomile from the

calming tea you've been sipping. If you can't taste anything, then say your favourite thing to taste.

Take another deep belly breath to end.

Breathe in for the count of four and breathe out for the count of six.

Place your right hand over your heart and send yourself love.

Finally...

Becoming so intimately reconnected with yourself and your thoughts holds the potential to change your life. Whether you feel you are a natural writer or not, please be reassured that there is no wrong way for you to write about your own thoughts and feelings. Whatever or however you choose to write, if you are writing from your heart, you can't go wrong.

Close your eyes and breathe.

Trust the process and give yourself this gift.

Allow yourself to let go.

It is your right to be heard and to fully express yourself.

It's time.

> *"Owning our story and loving ourselves through that process is the bravest thing that we will ever do"*
> – Brené Brown

Chloe Miller: 'We Overcome'

Our Story

I Have You
by K. Christy Moore

I will hold your hand, I will hold you
I will hear your story, I will see your pain
I will be your rock, I will be the plane
That flies you high above the world
Where turmoil lies

I will be your sister
While you sort through lies
I will be your back, your legs, your heart
I will give you hope for each new start
When days turn night
When you just can't sleep
I'll be there and keep
You safe from those things
Under your bed

I will hold your hand
I will hold you.

Ruth Woodcock: 'Helping Hands'

Women of Wisdom and Courage: Healing and Loving After Narcissistic Abuse

*"We are all connected and part of the tapestry
to ignite more healing"*
– Alex Martin

Needing to heal after an abusive relationship with a narcissist is one of the hardest things you'll ever have to go through. Women of Wisdom and Courage® was founded by Dr Sally Olewe-Richards, in October 2019, to provide women with an opportunity to access specialist support to heal, but more than that to create a safe, online space and sisterhood where women survivors can feel at home.

There is immense healing power through connecting to others, to feel we're heard without needing to share our own story. It is shining a light in the darkness that's been created, to remind ourselves of what is true. Our truth, our voice, our feelings are all valid and need to be expressed. As Brené Brown famously said, "Shame dies when stories are told in safe places".

"I feel so privileged to bear witness to so many women who tell their stories and for there to be a bond across the world with other souls who understand and respect the path of life so many of us have had to walk... having a place to voice, where validation is given, is a true gift.
– Women of Wisdom and Courage® online community member

Sally's vision for Women of Wisdom and Courage® is to provide women with the necessary support and guidance to heal, to create an empowering and safe online community, and long-term a movement for social justice and change. The name Women of Wisdom and Courage® captures what it means to survive and thrive after a narcissistic relationship and draws on The Serenity Prayer.

God, grant me serenity to accept the things I cannot change,
Courage to change the things I can,
And wisdom to know the difference.

We are never able to control the narcissist's behaviour, but we are able to change our reaction to it. By seeing the wisdom in controlling what we can and letting go of what we can't and finding the courage to take those next steps, we can begin our journey to healing.

We will never tell you to leave your relationship, or to stop loving that person; it is the most difficult thing to do. However, our sincere hope is that you discover the wisdom within you and see that taking back control in your life is always within your power. You are only ever one decision away from it. It takes courage and we are here to love you and guide you through that journey.

"This group has given me the soft space to land when I have fallen. I have experienced kindness in this group like nowhere else before. Unconditional."
−Women of Wisdom and Courage® online community member

The women contributors to this book have all walked the same path before you and you're not alone. Many of them are testament to the fact that we can decide to rewrite our story anytime we choose. By taking those first steps, you will gain immense inner wisdom and healing along the way, which one day you can pass on to other women who are standing where you are now.

Although the writing you may create, as a result of reading this book, is designed to support your own healing, you are invited to email your poetry to Women of Wisdom and Courage® to be featured on the website. The intention is to create a body of work from women survivors around the world, to raise awareness about the deeply damaging effects of narcissistic abuse and to give others hope that healing is possible.

Her Story. Your Story. Our Story.
Together, we're all Women of Wisdom and Courage.

Links and References

Links

To find out more and connect with Women of Wisdom and Courage®:

>   womenofwisdomandcourage.com

>   instagram.com/womenofwisdomandcourage

>   facebook.com/womenofwisdomandcourage

Email:
hello@womenofwisdomandcourage.com

To send your poems to be featured on the website:
poems@womenofwisdomandcourage.com

The domestic abuse charities being supported by sales of 'My Red Quilt'

Broxtowe Women's Project:
https://broxtowewomensproject.org.uk/

Fly Anyway Foundation:
https://www.iamthequeenbee.co.uk/flyanyway

More To Her Life:
https://www.moretoherlife.co.uk/

References

Hari, J. (2018) *The Lost Connections: Uncovering the Real Causes of Depression - And the Unexpected Solutions*, NY, USA: Bloomsbury

Koschwanez, H.E., Kerse, N., Darragh, M., Jarrett, P., Booth, R.J. and Broadbent, E. (2013) Expressive writing and wound healing in older adults: a randomized controlled trial, *Psychosom Med*, 75(6): 581-90

Lepore, S.J. and Smyth, J.M. (2002) *The Writing Cure: How Expressive Writing Promotes Health and Emotional Well-being*, Washington DC, USA: American Psychological Association

Myles, A. (2015) 'The Toxic Attraction Between an Empath and a Narcissist':
https://www.elephantjournal.com/2015/06/the-toxic-attraction-between-an-empath-a-narcissist/

Pennebaker, J.W. and Evans, J.F. (2014) *Expressive Writing: Words That Heal*, Enumclaw, WA, USA: Idyll Arbor

Suskin, J. (2020) *Every Day Is a Poem: Find Clarity, Feel Relief, and See Beauty in Every Moment*, Colorado, USA: Sounds True

Taylor, J. (2020) *Woman in Progress: The reflective journal for women and girls subjected to abuse and trauma*, Derby, UK: VictimFocus
https://www.victimfocus.org.uk/

Wride, M. (2020) The Song of Truth:
https://marywride.com/songoftruth/

About the Editors

Sally Olewe-Richards, PhD

Sally is the founder of Women of Wisdom and Courage®, the global sisterhood for healing from narcissistic abuse. She is a certified and ICF-approved One of Many® women's empowerment coach, specialising in supporting women to empower themselves to heal and go on to live their best lives. In Spring 2020, she piloted her research-evidenced and  trauma-informed programme, The L.O.V.E and H.E.A.L Method™ of Narcissistic Abuse Recovery with 45 women survivors.

Sally has always had a passion for social justice, volunteering in her teenage years for housing and citizen's rights charities. During her time as an undergraduate, at The University of York, Sally was an active member of women's groups and later taught on a domestic abuse module in the School of Sociology and Social Policy at The University of Nottingham.

As a social researcher, with a PhD background in sociology and social policy, she has worked for academic institutions, not-for-profit organisations and as a freelance consultant, covering a wide range of projects, from evaluating UK and international government policy through to programmes supporting people with multiple and complex needs involved in systems change work.

In April 2020, during the UK's first lockdown in response to the outbreak of Covid-19, Sally was invited to create and run the *Sisterhood Support: When Women Gather* project, to provide online support for women in Nottingham experiencing domestic abuse. In summer 2020, she was proud to become a trustee of the board and the incoming Treasurer of Broxtowe Women's Project, a local domestic violence charity supporting women and children.

Sally's vision for Women of Wisdom and Courage® is to create an empowering and safe online community, providing women with the necessary support and guidance to heal and rebuild their lives, and longer-term, an ambition for Women of Wisdom and Courage® to become a global movement for social justice and change.

Sally lives in her home city of Nottingham, England with her husband Nicholas and their two children.

Stephanie Kerber

Stephanie Kerber, an English poet and author, has been obsessed by the power and beauty of words since childhood. She wrote her first novel at the tender age of 14 as part of an English class and at 16 won her school's poetry competition, with a poem called "Famine". Social issues continue to feature in her poetry.

Stephanie contributed to an anthology of poetry called Poetic Wonders in 2019 and has published three novels, the Julie Diamond Trilogy, following the fortunes of Jules and Danny, musicians from Liverpool, who must overcome shadows from their pasts in order to build a future together. In December 2020, she released a book of her own poetry entitled "Down Moonlit Paths", based on themes of escape, freedom, adventure and nature.

Stephanie lives in Hertfordshire, England with her husband Richard and has two grown up daughters.

Printed in Great Britain
by Amazon

59142787R00108